*Crazy People Like Us*

*Crazy People Like Us: Love & Loss on the Other Side of the World*
by Harold Campbell

Copyright © 2021 Harold Campbell.

ISBN-13: 978-1737045090

Published by Lazarus Tribe Media
Rome, GA

Edited by Rachel Pennacchio

Cover Artwork by Maddison Umberger

Cover and Interior Design by Rachel Pennacchio

# CRAZY PEOPLE LIKE US

Love & Loss
on the
Other Side
of the
World

BY HAROLD CAMPBELL

Lazarus Tribe Media
Rome, GA

*To Rita,*
*May your mother's memory live forever*

# ACKNOWLEDGMENTS

Even before I returned to the United States, friends began nudging me to write a book about my experiences teaching English in Russia and India. Once I arrived back in the U.S., I tried two or three times to write it, but I could type only a page or two before painful, still-fresh memories overwhelmed me, and I had to stop.

When the COVID-19 lockdown began in Spring 2020, I decided to use the extra time at home to finally put the story on paper. My main purposes were to answer questions people asked me while I was living overseas and, most of all, to honor my wife, Nadya. I didn't follow any literary style. I didn't even come up with a title. Rather, I told the simple story while adding personal observations about life and culture in both India and Putin's Russia. I shared my draft with quite a few friends and family members, and they overwhelmingly responded that I should publish it.

Despite the enthusiastic reaction, I knew what I had written wasn't quite publishable. I read books and articles on how to write a memoir, I went through probably a half-dozen famous and not-so-famous memoirs for inspiration, and I asked for advice from already-published authors. I learned a lot from that, but when I contacted several publishers, I had no success.

I was about to give up when I met Rachel Pennacchio, owner of Lazarus Tribe Media, an independent publisher in Rome, Georgia. She saw a lot of promise in my work. She helped me transform it from a chronicle of my life overseas with a few observations added into a narrative that goes beyond everyday routine to exploring my thoughts and feelings in hopes that perhaps people can find meaning from my experiences.

It's a cliché, but there is no way I could have finished this project alone. As a first-time book author, I thank Rachel for her experience in the publishing world and for asking penetrating questions that helped me focus on turning this into something I hope will be compelling and engaging for readers. Thanks to Lenni Giacin for her enthusiasm and to David Brazzeal for lending some of his expertise gained through publishing his own book. I also appreciate the support from such former colleagues in the newspaper world as Susan Keaton, Cliff Morrison, Neal McChristy, and Bruce Crosby. In addition, I offer my sincere thanks to many friends and family members whose support kept me going when my batteries needed to be recharged.

In writing this book, I relied on notes I wrote while in Russia and India and on memory. All direct quotes are as I remember them, and no scenes or dialogue have been added for "dramatic effect." I have changed some names and details have for privacy. If you choose to keep on reading, I hope you enjoy the journey.

*Harold Campbell*
*October 2021*

# CONTENTS

# CONTENTS

# 1

# WELCOME TO RUSSIA

My first experience with Russian culture shock happened in a grocery store checkout line on a cold, early December evening in 2010. The place was St. Petersburg, Russia, the city where my Russian fiancée, Nadya, and I were planning to be married, and I was looking forward to teaching English. Only three days before, I boarded a Delta airliner in Kansas City, Missouri, where the sky was sunny, and the temperature was in the low 50s Fahrenheit. When I arrived in Moscow the next day, sunshine filled the sky, but the temperature was minus-6°F. Nadya met me at the airport, and we took an overnight train to her home in St. Petersburg.

On this evening, I needed a few things for the apartment where I had just moved in. However, Nadya was teaching her own English classes at the same time and couldn't come with me. For the first time, I was about to experience the local culture alone.

Frozen slush crunched beneath my boots as soon as I stepped outside the 18-floor apartment building where I had just moved in. A few minutes later, I stood at the entrance to one of the hundreds, maybe thousands, of small neighborhood groceries dotting St. Petersburg. The lights inside the store pierced the deepening twilight, which in early December in that part of Russia begins about 4 p.m. A vapor cloud escaped my lips as I exhaled and clasped the red metal door handle to enter. A slight twinge of nervousness pinched the inside of my stomach.

Melting snow and ice dripping from the soles of shoppers' boots left a slick, black film on top of the tile floor. I made a conscious effort to keep from falling, as one of the primary goals I maintained throughout my stay in Russia was to appear as inconspicuous as possible. The store was rectangular with narrow aisles and shelves crammed with boxes, bags, and plastic bottles, all labeled, of course, in Russian. Plastic containers of imported Heinz ketchup provided a reminder of back in the United States. At that time of day, shoppers (mainly middle-aged men) and *babushkas* (grandmothers or older women) nudged past, careful not to make eye contact. Most dressed in drab black or brown coats with scarves wrapped around their necks. All covered their heads from the cold outside, men with hats and women with either hats or scarves. More fashionably dressed young adults were still at work.

I only needed a few inexpensive things, and I managed to find them thanks mainly to photos on boxes and figuring out words from the Russian alphabet I had learned years earlier. Incidentally, one of the convenient things about stores in that part of the world is the price on the shelf is what you pay at the register—no guessing about how much to add for taxes.

There was no hurry, so I decided to explore a little longer. I checked out the freezer section. Missing were the ubiquitous boxes of waffles, microwave dinners, and frozen pizzas found in American groceries of any size. Instead, there were dozens of frozen fish, presumably from the nearby Gulf of Finland or Baltic Sea, and a variety of foods I wouldn't experience until later.

After that came a small produce section. A few fruits on display were imported from China or the Middle East, but mostly that part of the store was filled with boxes of cabbages, potatoes, and carrots, along with a smattering of garlic, cucumbers, mushrooms, tomatoes, and herbs. I imagined what American shoppers would think when examining potatoes or carrots still caked with dirt, while some of the potatoes were pocked with bruises or sprouts. I continued walking until I looked down to the end of the aisle where a big calico cat lounged on top of a heater. It turned out the cat lived in the store.

When I could delay no longer, I got in line at the lone cash register. After the few people in front of me paid for their items, my turn came. The cashier was an overweight, middle-aged woman whose face appeared frozen into a permanent scowl. Hunched over the register, she rang up my purchase, which didn't come to a lot of money. As I had just arrived in the country and exchanged some dollars for rubles, I still mainly had large bills. However, the look on her face told me she didn't want to make change for that much money. I showed her the smallest bill I had and even turned my pockets inside out to let her see for herself.

Yet, she showed no sympathy. Instead, her eyes narrowed, her facial muscles tightened, and she muttered something in Russian. As she counted the change, I walked the few feet to the end of the counter to bag my things. (Even the largest supermarkets are self-service in Russia.) Once I placed the last item in the plastic bag, she threw the change toward me. Bills fluttered in the air, and coins clanked on the metal countertop.

For one of the few times in my life, I was shocked. I tilted my head slightly and squeezed my lips together. My eyes focused on the back of the cashier, who continued to wait on customers standing in line. All the manners instilled in me growing up in Georgia and then as a young adult in Kansas and Nebraska failed to help me understand what had just happened. I shook my head and left the store. Through the frigid darkness, I trudged home.

A couple of hours later, when my soon-to-be-wife Nadya finished teaching her English classes for the day, I told her about my first solo visit to a St. Petersburg grocery store.

"Any cashier in North America who did that would have been fired on the spot," I said. Looking back, I realize how naïve I probably sounded.

Nadya sympathized with my American sensitivities, but she simply smiled and spoke the three words which summarized my life in the world's largest country: "Welcome to Russia."

I laughed, but part of me thought, "What am I getting myself into?" Over the next five and a half years – five years teaching English to teens and adults in Russia and five months helping teach children at two Christian orphanages in India – I found out. From the heights of love to the depths of grief, I experienced life outside the comfort zone and learned more about people, God, and myself.

# 2

# AN END AND A BEGINNING

Speaking the day after the attack on Pearl Harbor, President Franklin D. Roosevelt called December 7, 1941, "a date which will live in infamy." For me, December 1, 1993, carries the same significance.

On that cool, cloudy morning, my first wife, Mary, and I sat in a courtroom in Oberlin, Kansas, an agricultural town of 2,000 in northwest Kansas, to officially end our eight-year marriage. I felt dirty. I felt slimy. I felt like a failure as a husband, as a father, and as a Christian.

We had moved to Oberlin in the summer of 1991 after Mary finished her family practice residency at a hospital in Wichita, Kansas. Unlike many small towns, Oberlin still had a hospital and clinic. Considered by the state of Kansas as a medically underserved area, the city had a search committee always on the lookout for new physicians. With about a year and a half still left in her residency, Mary was recruited to be Oberlin's first woman doctor. Even before she and I and our two young children, Tim and Esther, relocated, Oberlin-area women started scheduling appointments with her.

Unfortunately, Mary and I had marital problems from the beginning. I admit my share of the blame, particularly when I ignored several "red flag" issues before and after the wedding. Instead, I dismissed them and thought maybe those who said I had been too picky back in my single days were right after all. I drove her cra-

15

zy with my passive-aggressiveness and default avoid-conflict-at-all-costs behavior. On the other hand, she cut me to the core with vicious words and constant criticism. I remember times inside our 1920s bungalow when she complained about how I cleaned the house, or when we were in a group and she would ignore me standing next to her. She could give other accounts about me, I'm sure. The more I appeased her or tried to draw boundaries, the angrier she became. We grew apart emotionally and spiritually. I stopped talking to her because no matter what I said, it seemed I was always wrong. I had hoped the Oberlin move would help. Instead, I felt abandoned and destroyed.

One night Mary and I lay in bed together. Neither one of us was asleep. The weight of all the emotions inside me grew unbearable. After tossing and turning for a few minutes, I walked to the bathroom and opened the medicine cabinet. Inside sat pill bottles ranging from Tylenol to various prescriptions. None contained anything lethal. To me, that didn't matter. I filled a plastic cup on the sink with water and gulped down every pill. I didn't want to die; I only wanted to ease the pain. I returned to bed. Not long after that, I felt nauseated. I returned to the bathroom and vomited into the toilet.

As I made my way back to the bedroom, I told myself to snap out of it. Our problems were solvable, or so I thought. I suggested counseling. We saw a counselor together once a week. Another day each week, I went by myself for help with anxiety and self-esteem. After about four months, however, Mary told me she thought I wasn't "getting better" and quit going. A short time later, she ordered me out of the house and started the paperwork for divorce. When I asked for her official reasons, she said because I "never did any work around the house" and neglected Tim and Esther.

Between the time we separated and when the divorce became final, I found a newspaper reporter position in Beatrice, Nebraska, about 220 miles north and east of Oberlin. My self-esteem grew with the help of supportive and positive co-workers. I also found a strong church with an active singles' group. I felt like I reached an oasis and jumped in the cool water after wandering for years in a desert.

The trial lasted no more than 30 minutes. My attorney advised me to remain calm and professional, but my voice cracked a couple of times when he asked me questions about the kids. Mary's attorney asked me why I hadn't given Esther a card for her fourth birthday a few days earlier. I answered I gave Esther a Barney game and

Tim a toy road grader and didn't think a card was necessary. The attorney looked at Mary to confirm the information. After Mary nodded her head, the attorney said, "No further questions." Seconds later, the judge ruled the marriage dissolved and said documents would be set up according to state law for visitation and distribution of property.

The legal process was over, but a gaping hole grew inside me. I missed my kids terribly, and I still hoped and prayed for reconciliation. It never happened. Mary and the children moved to where she came from in the Joplin, Missouri, area to work in the emergency room at a hospital. I found a job at the newspaper in Independence, Kansas, to be closer to Tim and Esther. Nothing else changed, however. About three years later, Mary remarried. The kids were excited; I was crushed. Any hope of reconciliation evaporated. At the time, it was the lowest point in my life. Some nights I even prayed, "Jesus, come sleep next to me." The day after one nighttime crying jag, I asked to see my pastor in his office. "I know all the right verses and all the right concepts," I told him with a shaking voice. "All my life, I've helped others, but now I'm the one who needs help."

God helped. I couldn't have made it without Him. In addition to supportive friends, He seemed closer than ever. Psalm 27 became a favorite, especially verses 13 and 14: "I remain confident in this: I will see the goodness of the LORD in the land of the living. Wait for the LORD; be strong and take heart and wait for the LORD." Another was Psalm 34:18: "The LORD is close to the brokenhearted and saves those who are crushed in spirit."

In terms of relationships, that was the way things stood for about 10 years. Occasionally, I considered dating again, but with my hectic and irregular work schedule, I didn't want to take away from the little time I had with the children. As they got older, the thought crossed my mind again. I took some steps in that direction, but I felt I was acting out of selfishness rather than for what was best for the other person and me. I finally concluded I wasn't meant to marry.

That began to change in September 2008. Although I was prepared to live the rest of my life single, I hadn't resigned myself to becoming a recluse. Instead, meeting new people and attempting new things were part of my strategy to keep away bitterness and self-pity. I was surfing the internet on one warm, sunny day when I was intrigued by a Christian pen-pals website I found. Unlike dating sites where romantic relationships were the goal, this was a place I thought I could make friends with people from different countries and cultures with no expectations of anything else.

The site had maps of the world where you could click on a country and a list of potential pen pals would appear, many with photos. One of the first countries I clicked on was Nepal. I found another Christian journalist living there who was fluent in English and emailed him. We became friends, and soon after that, he and his wife immigrated to New York City to work with a ministry to Nepalese immigrants. We still communicate often.

Next, I looked on the map and thought it would be interesting to talk with someone from Russia. I grew up during the Cold War when an American couldn't communicate with an average Russian, so I thought, why not? I clicked on Russia, and down came a long list of Russians seeking pen pals. Even though it was supposed to be a Christian website, many of the photos of young Russian women were on the revealing side.

However, I stopped when I came to the photo of a modestly dressed woman with dark eyes and a cute smile. Rather than a provocative pose, her face looked "friendly." Her name was Nadya. After thinking about it for a minute, I figured it would be no big deal to send her an email, so I composed a three- or four-sentence message introducing myself and asking her to tell me about herself and where she lived. I hoped for an answer but wasn't expecting one.

I woke up sometime in the middle of the night. Curiosity overcame me. I got out of bed, turned on my computer, and clicked on the link to my email. Sitting in my inbox was an email from Nadya. She wrote she was an English teacher who had a young daughter named Rita and was divorced. Her ex-husband, she said, was abusive, drank a lot, and "liked other girls better than me." I was surprised she was so open to me in the first email. It was the start of the open communication that marked our relationship – with a few exceptions – from the beginning. I didn't wait until morning to respond. Instead, I wrote back right away and asked her more questions about the city where she lived, where she attended church, and things that interested her. She answered the next day and included another photo. From that point on, we contacted each other almost daily until we were married a little over two years later.

Not long before our wedding date, Nadya told me my second message was what sparked her interest in me. "I got messages from a lot of men," she said. "But you were the only one who was really interested in me as a person. All the other men just said crazy things."

In the beginning, I felt a little like a teenager with a crush. It was hard to concentrate or fall asleep, and I read her emails over and over. Distance and the 11-hour time difference between us didn't matter. If you drew a line on a globe from where I lived in Kansas north to the North Pole and back down the other side, you would end up close to Nadya's home in Siberia. There were moments, however, when I thought this new long-distance relationship was crazy. In the past, I often succumbed to some inner pressure in my mind to back away from risk. There were the girls I never asked out because I was afraid of rejection. There were career paths I might have taken, but I never took them because I feared failure. On the other hand, there were other times in my life when I overcame negative self-talk and comments from others to step out in faith because I knew it was the right thing for me. Nadya's messages were encouraging, funny, and thoughtful. In just a few weeks, she had already made enough of an impact in my life that I couldn't let anything I did or thought drive her away. Perhaps this time, the risk would be worth it.

Right away, we learned we had lots in common and, at the same time, our differences complemented each other. Nadya called herself a "quick gale" because of her rapid changes in emotion and said I was her "calm sea" because of what she thought of as my quiet strength and stability. I replied she couldn't see the water churning beneath my supposedly placid surface. We shared many more similarities, however, especially in faith and values. We retained our beliefs in core Christian doctrines, but we were disillusioned with many of the trappings and squabbles found in institutional religion. We seemed to view the world through the same combination of idealism mixed with reality. Our main goal was to share God's love with everyone we could. Not long after we met, Nadya told me about a Christian book she had read, *Moments with the Savior* by Ken Gire, and asked if I would like to read it together. Of course, I agreed, and we talked about a chapter each Saturday morning my time. I also mailed her some Christian books that meant a lot to me, especially *The Pursuit of God* by A.W. Tozer, and she liked them.

Meanwhile, I was looking for a change from my newspaper job. The effects of online media were leading to downsizing and job insecurity in the journalism world. According to several sources, the number of newspaper newsroom jobs dropped from a high of 56,400 in 2000 to 41,500 in 2010 and continued declining. Daily newspaper circulation plummeted by more than 25 million subscribers in the first two decades of the 2000s, while advertising revenue went from $37.8 billion in 2008 to $14.3 billion in 2018.

For me, newsroom downsizing meant I was now doing the work three or four people would have done when I first started as a reporter. In addition, I had already been downsized twice myself. I thought of alternatives to being laid off again.

An option I considered was getting a master's degree in English with an English as a Second Language certification because I had always felt a sense of fulfillment in helping people from other countries learn English. An ESL certification would allow me to teach in American public schools, but most states and school districts require a master's degree in education combined with a specific training program and extensive practice teaching. At my age, I didn't want to go into a lot of debt getting another degree.

I told Nadya about my situation, and she said there was no reason for me to spend thousands of dollars on a degree. Instead, I could get a TEFL certification online for a fraction of the cost of attending a university. A TEFL certification from a reputable organization would enable me to teach English in countries where English is not the main language, as well as for various paid and volunteer teaching positions for immigrants through private language schools, community organizations, and other educational institutions in the U.S. On top of that, she said there was tremendous demand in Russia for certified native English-speaking teachers with college degrees. I had never considered living and working in Russia, but I didn't want to look back in 10 or 20 years and regret not taking the opportunity.

For at least an hour every Sunday through Friday evening (my time), we talked by Skype. We had long talks on Saturday morning when we spent two to three hours together. Whether we were talking about a serious subject or just joking around, I felt comfortable with her. She seemed to think the same about me.

Over time, I found out more about her. Nadya (short for Nadezhda, the Russian word for "hope") was born in 1972 in a village near Krasnodar in the Kuban region of southern Russia. She, her parents, and two sisters lived in a small wooden house that featured a garden, an outdoor well, and a variety of livestock. I never learned much about her family's background, although Nadya told me her family had been *kulaks*, wealthier peasants who owned property and were the objects of Stalin's forced collectivization program in the 1930s. Some of her relatives, she said, likely ended up in the gulag. One day during the Nazi invasion of the Soviet Union in World War II, one of Nadya's grandmothers was working in her garden. Suddenly, a German tank rumbled from out of nowhere and ran over her. She died instantly.

Like almost all Soviet-era youths, Nadya attended government schools and belonged to the Young Pioneers, the Soviet version of the Scouts. Each day included a political lesson from someone representing the Communist Party. Nadya estimated she was one of the 95 percent in her school who didn't care about politics, so she rarely listened. Much later, I saw photos of Nadya as a child and young adult. She was usually smiling, such as in the photo of her at age 3 or 4 holding a fishing pole with a small fish on the line or the photo of the kindergarten class she taught after graduating college.

However, her mother, Nina, and stepfather, Victor, weren't happy with the financial prospects of living in a small agricultural village. When Nadya was 10, the family moved to Nizhnevartovsk, a city of about 250,000 in western Siberia near one of the world's largest oil fields. Winter temperatures there regularly reach minus-40 or 50. Snow in June is not unusual. Her parents hoped they could make good money living in an oil city, but things didn't work out that way. High-paying jobs never came. On top of that, an economic crisis coincided with the collapse of the Soviet Union. While the 1990s were booming economic times for many in the United States, they were hard times in Russia. After the Russian government devalued the ruble, pensions and savings evaporated overnight, and store shelves emptied. Nadya shared a coat with a friend because that was all they could afford. Nizhnevartovsk women wore the same three styles of dresses because those were the only styles available in shops.

Nadya, meanwhile, went to university and became a kindergarten teacher. Although she loved children, she didn't care much for the bureaucracy and paperwork associated with teaching and decided to change careers. While in high school and university, Nadya took English classes. She both loved it and excelled at it, and after she left kindergarten teaching, she began teaching English at a private language school in Nizhnevartovsk.

In December 1991, when the Soviet Union dissolved and the Russian Federation was formed, Nadya got married. She and her husband had a daughter, Margarita (known as "Rita"), but a terrible marriage. Nadya's husband was an abusive alcoholic who openly cheated on her. I never pried into the facts of her previous marriage unless she brought the subject up, but one time she described how he once opened the refrigerator door and shoved her head inside. She kept many other painful memories to herself.

Nadya managed to successfully file for divorce, rare at the time in patriarchal Russia, but her life spiraled downward afterward. Her troubles related mainly to problems between her and her ex-husband and mother-in-law. I can't remember all the details, but according to the divorce agreement, they put the apartment they had shared in Rita's name. This hindered Nadya in the future, especially when applying for a tourist visa to leave the country and for various legal matters in Russia. Nina took the ex-husband's side in the divorce and somehow kicked Nadya and Rita out of the apartment. Nadya and Rita managed to find other places to stay, but they returned to the apartment after her mother went to live in the small town of Petrovsky near Krasnodar. Despite all this, Nadya never harbored any bitterness toward her mother.

Another point of contention between Nadya and her mother stemmed from religion. Nadya's mother was a devout Russian Orthodox who believed anything besides Orthodoxy was heresy. Nadya, however, became disenchanted with what she saw as the legalism and ritualism involved in the Russian Orthodox faith. As she put it, she grew exhausted trying to remember all the do's and don'ts. One day at a bus stop in Nizhnevartovsk, she met a woman -- a member of another church in town -- who told her about a faith based on grace, not works. Nadya attended the woman's church, and at first, everything went well. She decided to trust Christ with her life, and she was hired as one of three church secretaries.

However, the church focused on how to be healthy and wealthy rather than serving others. Nevertheless, she convinced the church leaders to let her start a telephone helpline and staff it with volunteers to take calls from alcoholics, drug addicts, or anyone else who called for assistance. Although the ministry helped many people, the pastor and elders voted to discontinue it because it had brought in no new members or donations.

She felt empty not only because of a lack of Bible study but also because women's meetings usually centered on such topics as what colors best match your complexion, and, like many Russian church-es, the pastor looked upon as a tsar. One weekend conference, for example, was devoted to lessons on "How to serve your pastor." For Nadya, the worst came when the church rejected Rita. As a teen-ager, Rita began to follow the punk culture, with its unique clothing and musical styles, and wore her hair in a mohawk. Her appear-ance upset the staid church members and staff, who began to insult her and question Nadya's motherhood qualifications. Nadya was searching for acceptance and something deeper than her church could provide.

Then I came along.

Even as far back as elementary school, I was interested in things like history, government, cultures, and languages. One of my prized possessions was a shortwave radio, which in those pre-in-ternet days of the 1960s and 1970s was the only way to listen to sta-tions from other countries. Before school, almost every day in sixth grade, I listened to Radio Australia, while I had my first taste of Canadian comedy with Royal Canadian Air Farce on Radio Canada International. Especially interesting was hearing the English-lan-guage broadcasts from Radio Moscow.

Language had always interested me, which was a major reason I had already decided by the time I was in junior high school that I wanted to be either a newspaper or broadcast journalist. Because I thought I could write better than I talked, I chose newspaper jour-nalist. I was also probably one of the only students in high school who looked forward to the foreign language requirement. I really wanted to learn Russian, not only because of my interest in Russian history and culture but also because of a Cold War fascination with life behind the Iron Curtain. However, the chances of a high school in north Georgia offering Russian classes in the 1970s were zero. My next choice was French, but it was only offered during band. I had been in the band since fifth grade, and I knew I couldn't quit for just a French class. As a result, I took Spanish for two years in high school and two years in college and really enjoyed it. Years lat-er, I was in a McDonald's in suburban Kansas City when I gave my order to a Latino man working at the counter. He said it would be a few minutes, and I answered in Spanish, *"No hay prisa."* ("There's no hurry.") Apparently, that simple act of speaking a few words to him in his native language touched him. When my order was ready, he had a serious expression on his face and spoke to me barely above a whisper, *"Vaya con Dios."*

That is only one example of how I have always enjoyed meeting people from other countries. One of my best friends in high school was a doctor's son from Ecuador named Walter. Walter wanted to be an engineer and was a walking calculator. In fact, some of my other friends and I nicknamed him "Tex" for "Texas Instruments." In exchange for helping me with math and Spanish, I helped him with English and history. In junior college, I met a pair of students from Iran. We met just before the Islamic revolution, and they feared telling me too much in case an informant overheard our conversation and told the secret police. I took them seriously.

While I was in junior college, my father's work transferred him to the company's headquarters on the Kansas side of the Kansas City metropolitan area. For most of my life, I had planned on majoring in journalism at the University of Georgia. However, the idea of living in a different part of the country and attending the highly-rated University of Kansas journalism school appealed to me, and I decided to finish my last two years of college there.

In my first year, I had a work-study job in what was then called the university's Foreign Student Office. All incoming international students had to check in there at the start of each semester, and others came in to get immigration or other documents approved. Many international students also lived in my dormitory. On move-in day one semester, I went down to the lobby to try out my mailbox combination. Standing beside me, a Japanese student couldn't figure out how to open his. I showed him, and I gained an instant friend. He occasionally invited me to his room for some Japanese food sent by his family back home.

Sometimes friendships with students from other countries took on more serious aspects than unlocking mailboxes, however. During my college days in the late 1970s, more international students at U.S. universities came from Iran than from any other country. As Iran entered its Islamic revolution and radicals stormed the U.S. embassy in Tehran and took hostages, scuffles broke out on many campuses between Iranian students protesting the shah's regime and American counter-protesters. Many walls on my campus had anti-Iranian and anti-Muslim graffiti scribbled on them. I lived across the hall from an American student and his Iranian roommate. The Iranian student was short and thin, and his face was locked in a perpetual smile. He was one of the friendliest people I knew. As the situation worsened, the American student and I decided to hide his roommate in a storage area above my closet if violence broke out in the dormitory. As I lived alone, no one else would know. Fortunately, we never needed to follow through on our plan.

One of the results of all my interactions with people from other nations in these early years showed me that behind our political and cultural differences, we were all individuals. From my perspective, people from all over the world shared such common goals as getting a good education, finding a stable career, and providing for their families. It didn't matter whether they were from Latin America, Japan, Iran, or anywhere else.

The summer between my junior and senior years of college, I became a Christian. Following that, I became involved in missions to learn to share this Gospel I now embraced with people both near and far. The first way I learned to share was through prayer. Without a strong inner life, there is no strong outer life. The second way became giving. For example, around the time the Iron Curtain fell, although money for my first wife and me was tight, I donated to send Bibles to Russia and Eastern Europe. It just seemed like the right thing to do. The third way became volunteering. For a few years in the late 1990s, I volunteered in the communications department of the U.S. office for Voice of the Martyrs, an international organization that helps Christians around the world living under persecution. The descriptions of what Christ-followers in other parts of the world must endure made many of the complaints from American Christians seem puny. One Sunday evening at my church, I gave a talk on Christian persecution. When it was over, the music director said, "Well, you've made us all uncomfortable."

"Good," I responded with a smile. "That's what I wanted to do."

Still, I desired to do more. After my unwanted divorce, I concluded to make the rest of my life count. At the same time, I could sense I was supposed to live in another country at some point, although I didn't know where. I also didn't want to go until after Tim and Esther became adults.

Because my ex-wife was a doctor and I was a newspaper reporter who had been Mr. Mom with the children, I got a little bit of money from the divorce settlement. With some of it, I bought an airplane ticket to a place I had always wanted to visit, Montreal. Exploring the old city and experiencing the Quebec culture were part of the reason I went, but I also wanted to see if there were any opportunities to serve in ministry there in the future. On my last night in Montreal, I looked out the window to my bedroom at the bed and breakfast where I stayed toward the cross on top of Mont Royal. "Someday, I'll be back," I prayed.

Some day came almost seven years later. In those pre-9/11 days, when the internet was new, people could look up the names of Southern Baptist International Mission Board missionaries by country, except when they had to be kept secret due to security reasons. One day just after New Year in 2000, I decided to see if anyone was serving in Quebec. Back in the 1980s, I had written to the then-Canadian Southern Baptist offices in the Calgary area and got a "don't call us; we'll call you" response. However, this time was different. It turned out there was someone in the Montreal area, David Brazzeal, IMB strategy coordinator for Quebec, so I sent him a short email introducing myself and expressing my interest in learning more about the ministry in Quebec.

David returned my email almost immediately. He was especially intrigued by my job as a newspaper reporter because he realized the importance of good communications in ministry. His response surprised me because many Christians I knew asked me, "How can you be a Christian and a journalist?" I usually said something like, "How can you be a Christian and a plumber or a used car salesman?" David and I emailed almost every day for the next couple of months and found out we were on the same spiritual wavelength and shared many of the same quirks. He invited me to visit him and his family that summer. I went and became the Southern Baptist communications and prayer coordinator for Quebec and eastern Ontario. I wrote articles and performed other work to publicize the ministry and spiritual needs there, which included traveling to Montreal at least once a year.

This went on for almost ten years. I loved Montreal and Canada in general. One of the Montreal ministry leaders and his wife said I was their favorite U.S. visitor because they didn't have to explain everything to me. Some of my Canadian friends said I was the most "Canadian" American they had ever known, while others said the Canadian government should go ahead and give me citizenship. They joked that I could get an application at any Tim Horton's bakery, but I would have to ask the cashier. At the time, I would have gladly moved to Montreal, but no door ever opened. Meanwhile, many of the people I worked with in Quebec moved away, and I realized my involvement with Canada was ending.

It was also when Nadya came along.

After communicating daily for two or three months, Nadya and I reached the same conclusion: we needed to meet in person to answer whether our relationship was real or fantasy? Nadya first suggested I could fly to Nizhnevartovsk and stay with her and Rita in their apartment. That idea sounded good to me, but the process for a foreigner to get a Russian homestay visa puts a lot of responsibility on the host, and the traveler doesn't learn if the visa is approved until a few days before the trip. A better option was to meet in Ukraine. American citizens still don't need a visa to visit there as a tourist, and in those days before the current conflict in eastern Ukraine, Russian citizens didn't need one, either. Nadya had a good friend in the capital city, Kyiv, who was glad for us to stay with her in her apartment. I made reservations to fly to Kyiv for a week in late May 2009.

The day came. I boarded a non-stop flight in Kansas City for John F. Kennedy International Airport in New York and then another non-stop flight from JFK to Boryspil International Airport in Kyiv. Sitting next to me on the Kansas City to JFK flight was a Ukrainian woman living in Kansas City who would also be on the same flight to Kyiv. I told her I was glad she was there in case anything unexpected happened, but we encountered no problems.

As the plane landed in Kyiv, the reality hit me that I was about to meet Nadya in person for the first time. After all those months, I was ready. All of us on the flight passed quickly to the luggage carousel and through passport control. Rolling my bag behind me, I took a deep breath and walked through the exit to the terminal. Nadya was standing there, waiting.

She made her way as fast as she could through the crowd and reached me before I could take more than a few steps toward her. She was even more beautiful than the photos she emailed me showed. I looked down toward her and saw her shoulder-length dark hair and brown eyes and the soft smile that would melt me so many times in the future.

"Are you really here?" Nadya asked.

Without waiting for an answer, she pressed her head against my chest and embraced me. In turn, I held her tightly. Even though she was about six or eight inches shorter than me, my arms fit perfectly around her. We lingered there for a second or two before we left the terminal and boarded a commuter train to take us to the main part of town where Nadya's friend lived. The driver was talking to someone on the sidewalk outside, and no one else was aboard, so Nadya and I took advantage of the opportunity to have our first kiss. Nadya seemed to enjoy it. I know I did.

It was late morning. Except for a few fluffy clouds, a warm spring sun was the only thing in the clear blue sky. The train took us past rows of office and apartment buildings before crossing a large bridge over the wide Dnieper River. In the distance stood many churches with their distinctive domes and older structures that survived World War II.

After our first few minutes together, I began to feel like I had known Nadya forever. I was relaxed with her. We dropped off my bag at the apartment and toured some of the city. We did much the same the next morning and afternoon before we went to see a performance of *The Nutcracker* ballet that evening. Before the trip, Nadya had suggested going to it, and I agreed. I had never seen a ballet before, but I figured if I had the chance to see a professional production of a Tchaikovsky work anywhere near his neck of the woods, I should take advantage of it. The music and choreography were amazing, but not as incredible as Nadya in her blue dress sitting next to me.

Then something changed.

I didn't find out until after I arrived in Kyiv that some good friends of Nadya's, Anatoly and his wife, Maria, along with their friend, Vladimir, were going to pick us up on our third day there and drive us to Vladimir's home in Dniepropetrovsk (now Dnipro), a city of close to one million in central Ukraine about 300 miles southeast of Kyiv. Anatoly had been assistant pastor of Nadya's church in Nizhnevartovsk but recently became director of an orphanage ministry in India. Vladimir, whom Anatoly described as his best friend, pastored a church in Dniepropetrovsk. Nadya and I were supposed to spend three days with them, then return to Kyiv by train for our last two days together before my return flight to the U.S.

On the way to his home, Vladimir kept asking questions about what I had done in life. No matter what I answered, he criticized it. It was annoying, but it didn't upset me. Later at his apartment, he ended up insulting my pastor and even the study Bible I brought. In my American way of thinking, that was no way to treat a guest. But I wasn't back home.

At the same time, something happened with Nadya. From warm and caring, almost instantly, she became cold and distant. I asked her something about the TEFL certification class I was taking, but she ignored me. She snapped at me while I was ordering at a restaurant where all of us were eating. Once, I sat next to her on the couch, but she slid away from me. She acted friendly to the others, but to me, her eyes and face looked hard. Inside, my thoughts were angry, hurt, and confused. I had no idea what caused this abrupt change in her.

Before my trip, Anatoly asked me to speak at Vladimir's church one night when we were there, and Nadya would interpret. When the time came, I really didn't want to go. I had a talk prepared, but I couldn't concentrate enough to say anything coherent in my frame of mind. Even now, I can't remember a word I said. Nadya interpreted, but she stood four or five feet from me with her arms crossed and never looked at me. Her voice sounded irritated. I ended up speaking for only 10 minutes because I couldn't utter another syllable. After my talk, I watched an uncomfortable video Vladimir had put together about what appeared to be a survivalist camp that supposedly helped people become better Christians. The worst part of the presentation was when the video singled out a woman who had difficulty performing some of the camp's physical demands. What kind of Twilight Zone had I been transported to?

I seriously considered returning to Kyiv and seeing if I could either get an earlier flight or find a hotel room and enjoy my last two nights there alone. But for the time being, I kept my thoughts bottled up. Anatoly and Vladimir seemed to have no idea what was going on, and we all went bowling and to a movie together. They even gave Nadya and me the money to return to Kyiv on an overnight train. It was my first trip in a sleeper car, but the combination of the rattling from the tracks and my concern about Nadya kept me awake almost all night.

When we got to the apartment, Nadya told her friend about what had happened. The friend did her best to keep the peace and led us on a walking tour of some of the city's most beautiful and historical parts. At least, I got to check the site of the 11th century Great Gate of Kyiv off my bucket list and saw some stones from a church building dating from 500 AD. After that, Nadya and I spent time alone together without her friend. We sat in the middle of Independence Square with its 200-foot victory column in the distance, and I told her my point of view to everything that happened in the other city.

"I didn't come halfway around the world to see you and then be treated like your little internet friend," I said.

She said she understood, and her voice and face started to soften. We walked to another park, where I gave her a ring I bought for her before the trip. She smiled at me for the first time in three days. Later, she told me more about what was going through her mind at the time. She didn't give a lot of specifics, but she explained she had been under spiritual attack and wasn't herself. I agreed with that part. As she seemed to warm to me again, I didn't feel the same urge to leave as I did a day or two earlier. However, I was still a little unsure of where we stood.

Our last day together in Kyiv went well. She appeared to return to normal, and I felt more comfortable around her. My return flight left the following morning, and Nadya accompanied me on the commuter train to the airport. We stood just outside the security area. It would be the last time I could hold her and look into her eyes in no telling how long, so I was in no hurry. Finally, I could wait no longer, and we pried ourselves apart. Nadya stayed in Kyiv for a few more days and, in time, told me she cried all the way from the airport to the apartment.

Sitting in the boarding area, I decided to put those three days in Dniepropetrovsk behind me. For one, Nadya tried to explain what happened, and she didn't seem to want to end the relationship. Two, although no one would have blamed me for packing up and going home, I just couldn't do it. Besides, I realized there would likely come a time when she would have to forgive me for something big. Three, I loved her. She was my biggest fan. If I needed any encouragement, she would say something like, "You are the greatest. You must believe that." She listened to me and took me seriously. On top of that, she cared for me enough that she wouldn't let me slide back into the self-protective shell where I had spent much of my life. Because I knew she loved me, her words never came across as nagging. Instead, she made me a better person. How could I throw that away? Someone as special as her deserves a second chance, I reasoned.

As soon as I got back to my apartment, we talked again and took a moment to review our week together. Most of the time, however, we talked about our future together. The word "marriage" came up when Nadya stopped to ask, "Is this a proposal?"

"I suppose it is," I said.

"Then the answer is yes!"

The next question was, where would the wedding take place? Earlier, Anatoly invited Nadya to teach English to the children at the orphanage, but the paperwork and cost of getting married in India were exorbitant. It was the same in other countries. It turned out that the procedure and paperwork for us to be married in Russia would be less than in the U.S. But not by much.

For months, we collected papers and documents to prove to the satisfaction of the Russian government that we were who we said we were, and there was no legal barrier preventing us from being married. I had to supply such papers as a certified copy of my birth certificate, divorce decree, and passport photo page. Each had to be certified by the Kansas secretary of state's office and then sent to Russia. I am certain Nadya's paperwork mountain was even higher than mine.

The problem was Nadya and I didn't want to wait until the wedding to see each other again. I suggested she could visit me in the U.S. She thought it was a great idea. To get her tourist visa, she had to travel 1,000 miles from Nizhnevartovsk to the American consulate in Yekaterinburg, a city in the Urals region. We talked while she was on the train traveling across the frozen countryside on the clear winter night. Her description of the moonlight shining on the snow and birch trees along the tracks sounded like something out of *Doctor Zhivago*. She arrived at Yekaterinburg and went right away to the consulate. She didn't have to wait long to see an immigration official, but once she sat down at the official's desk, he only stared at his computer screen and told her, "Denied."

"Why?" Nadya asked.

"There's not enough proof that you'll return to Russia. Until there is a change in your circumstances, don't bother applying again." He explained Nadya didn't have ownership of her apartment and didn't have enough money in her bank account. The entire meeting lasted no more than two minutes.

Nadya was devastated. She told me she felt like the United States had rejected her. In the same city where the Bolsheviks executed the Romanov family in 1918, her dream of visiting the U.S. died. When I heard about what happened, I was incredulous. Nadya is no terrorist and wants to enter the country legally, I thought. I felt no better when I researched and discovered it was difficult for single Russian women to get visas to many western countries. The fear seemed to be that the women would marry western men only for their money, gain permanent residency, divorce them, and be able to stay legally. A woman lawyer from Moscow who I helped with English online was even denied a tourist visa to visit London on vacation. Nadya, one of the least materialistic people I had ever known, realized I didn't have a lot of money. Nevertheless, that made no difference in immigration law.

While we wrestled with paperwork and bureaucracy, we also spent a lot of time doing our pre-marital counseling. We read such books as *The Five Love Languages* by Gary Smalley and discussed how we could relate them to our future marriage. An exercise we did a lot was to ask how the other person would react to different scenarios. Any subject was fair game. For example, she asked me what she should do if I were in a bad mood and, like many males, retreated to myself. I assured her I wouldn't go far and I would return from my cave as soon as possible. I asked her once what should I do during her monthly period? From her answer, I understood I had better keep my distance as much as possible.

One book we read told women they should always look immaculate for their man. Nadya assured me she would wake up every morning at 4 o'clock to start getting ready for me to see her. Part of this might have come from the patriarchal society in which she grew up. A 2016 study, "Fast-Tracked or Boxed In? Informal Politics, Gender, and Women's Representation in Putin's Russia," said that although the participation of women in Russian politics has increased, this has not led to more equality for women overall. A controversial law passed in 2017 decriminalized first-time domestic abuse cases. This decision might explain why I once saw a man in a metro station yell at a woman and smack her in the face while waiting for a train.

I told Nadya I didn't agree with everything in that book, and she didn't have to get out of bed before sunrise because she always looked beautiful to me. After we were married and I saw how much she relished every moment of sleep she could get, I laughed to myself whenever I remembered this.

Another time, Nadya had a question I had to think about before answering: "What kind of wife do you want me to be?"

I asked her what she meant, and she said she wanted to know what she should do after we were married. I paused for a moment and reflected on what she experienced in her first marriage. Inside my heart, I could sense a little of her pain. I wanted to assure her she had my complete support.

"After we're married," I said, "you'll have a big playground. There will be a few boundaries like any married couple would have, but other than that, you can do whatever you want. I want you to be the person God made you to be, and I'll do whatever I can to help."

Nadya had never heard anything like that from a man. She was silent as tears welled up in her eyes. I think she would have kissed me if we hadn't been half a world apart.

At the same time, she experienced other changes in her life. Rita tired of her treatment at church and in Nizhnevartovsk in general and moved to St. Petersburg, where she would learn to be a cosmetologist. Nadya, meanwhile, was having more church problems. Along with a small group of other members, the church essentially excommunicated her for questioning some of the pastor's actions. Many of the people she thought were friends abandoned her, and others openly criticized her. We prayed and talked about that a lot until she decided to follow Rita and move to St. Petersburg herself. She was sure both of us could find teaching jobs there.

A short time later, all the marriage paperwork was submitted and approved. My Russian visa application was also submitted and approved. Ticket in hand, I boarded a plane for Russia. The date was December 1, 2010 – exactly 17 years after the divorce trial that officially ended my first marriage.

# 3

# THE WEDDING SURPRISE

For the past nine hours, a window seat in a Delta airliner served as my home. As the plane started its descent to Sheremetyevo International Airport in Moscow, I focused on the ground below. For someone who grew up in the Cold War and thought of Russia as an intriguing place locked behind a supposedly impenetrable Iron Curtain, it felt strange to see the snow-covered trees and hills below. Still, I had come this far, and nothing was going to stop me from marrying Nadya and beginning my teaching career. Yet, in Russia and elsewhere, sometimes the smallest things can create unexpected complications. The ink had not dried on our wedding documents when Nadya and I experienced that.

The part I had been dreading came soon after the plane landed: my encounter with Russian customs at the passport control window. At one extreme, I couldn't help having a vision of Cold War-era interrogations in some dark, smoky room with a single light bulb dangling from the ceiling at the end of a thin electrical cord. The reality, however, was the other extreme. The customs officer, a middle-aged, brown-haired woman in a blue uniform, simply stared at my passport, found my visa inside, glanced at me, typed something on her computer, stamped my passport, and slid it back to me through a small opening in the window. No words escaped her lips, and no change came to her stoic expression. I had experienced more trouble entering Canada on some of my trips there. Breathing a silent sigh of relief, I thought to myself, "Is that all?"

Fortunately, airport signs were in both Russian and English, so I found the door leading to the terminal waiting area. As I walked through the entryway, I was mobbed by a half-dozen taxi drivers seeking passengers. Ignoring them, I soon found Nadya waiting. A year and a half had passed since our meeting in Ukraine, but seeing her smile made the minus-6°F temperature outside more bearable. She had told me before that I could fly to Moscow instead of St. Petersburg because it would be cheaper and Delta had a non-stop flight from Atlanta to Moscow. We would meet there and then take the train from Moscow to St. Petersburg.

First, though, we took a commuter train from the airport to somewhere in the center of Moscow. Tourism wasn't the point of this visit, however. When we reached our stop, we had to find the travel office that prepared the invitation for my visa application so I could pay for it. I soon realized that although my clothes, coat, and boots were more than sufficient for Kansas winters, they posed no match for Russian cold and snow. Negotiating slick sidewalks with my luggage and an icy wind cutting through me turned out to be a challenge. We finished our errand, however, and after eating at a small café, we went to the Leningradsky railway station where we would board our train to St. Petersburg. The station, built in the 19th century, was undergoing renovations, and, amazingly, there was no heat in the passenger waiting area. It felt like sitting inside a freezer.

The train left at about 10 p.m. for our eight-hour, 400-mile trip. I wish I remembered more, but by this point, my brain and internal clock were out of order. Now, Russian Railways operates a high-speed passenger train between Moscow and St. Petersburg, but then everything was still an old-style slow train.

My immersion in Russian culture started here. Although there are first- (called "luxe") and second-class (called "cupe") cabins with private- and semi-private rooms, they are much more expensive, so we took what is called a "platzkart" (or third-class) car. The best way to describe a platzkart is a dormitory on wheels. Each car has 54 bunks, four on one side of a narrow aisle and two on the other. The side bunks are over and under the window, and the lower bunk can fold out to make a table. Passengers share one bathroom (when it's in order), and there is absolutely no privacy. On a future train trip, I told Nadya the lack of privacy in a platzkart would overwhelm many Americans.

Each ticket has a bunk assignment on it. That night, I had the top bunk above Nadya. For overnight trips, on top of each bunk sits a pillow, blanket, and a clear plastic package containing sheets and the special Russian-style pillowcase I could never figure out how to fit over the pillow correctly. A small towel and washcloth hang on the wall next to the bunk. Nadya, well, almost, never lost her patience with her clueless American fiancé, however, and showed me the tricks of how to prepare a platzkart bunk for sleeping. The problem was I couldn't sleep. For one thing, on the top bunk, I felt like my nose was only inches from the ceiling, plus the bunk was so narrow I thought it would be just like me to fall off, break my neck on the floor below, and die, all on my first night in Russia. The other thing was the reporter instinct in me wanted to observe and absorb all I could, even though I felt beyond exhausted. The muffled whispers from other passengers in a language I didn't understand. The staccato rhythm of the wheels. The snow and slender birch trees lining the tracks. All of those sights and sounds passed through my head before I finally drifted off. My little nap didn't last much more than an hour, not enough for the day ahead.

Sunrise was still a couple of hours away as the train pulled into St. Petersburg's Moskovskaya station, once the official railroad station for the tsars. Before we reached the city, the snow had started to fall more heavily, and I had seen from the platzkart window that it was getting deeper. The temperature hadn't increased, either.

Nadya carried her stuff as I rolled my bag along the icy sidewalk from the rail platform to the Mayakovskaya metro station next door. The time was approaching 7 a.m., and a steady stream of workers passed through the entrance doors to start the daily trip to their jobs. It wasn't the ideal time for a Russia- neophyte like me to take the St. Petersburg metro for the first time. With hardened, impatient faces behind me, I managed to get myself and my luggage through the turnstile and make it to the long escalator down to the platform. Once the next train arrived, we made our way to the section of St. Petersburg where Nadya and Rita lived, an area known as Vasilyevsky Ostrov (or "Vasily's Island"). When we reached the right station, we exited and took the 15-minute walk to the apartment. The combination of jet lag, sleeplessness, and general cluelessness blurred most of my memory of those first moments in St. Petersburg.

Darkness and an icy fog still shrouded the city. The snow- and ice-covered sidewalks were lined with bookstores, clothing shops, and restaurants (including a Pizza Hut and KFC) in buildings dating from the late 1800s and early 1900s, but anything I saw in the feeble dawn looked drab and gray. (The buildings appeared much nicer in sunlight.) By this time, Nadya was rightfully getting a little impatient with me as she was also tired from the trip. I was holding her up trying to keep my bag rolling steadily on the uneven, ice-glazed walkways.

Finally, we arrived at the apartment building. In time, seeing such buildings became commonplace, but I tried to take in as much as I could while still attempting to keep up with Nadya. Shaped like a U, the conrete buildling stood seven or eight stories tall and was coated with a dark yellow paint that looked like someone had left a big smudge on it. A large stone fence taller than an adult, also painted yellow, separated the building from the sidewalk. We passed through an arched entryway into a small courtyard called a *dvor*. There are thousands of similar courtyards all over St. Petersburg. When we reached the correct building, Nadya pressed the numbers on a keypunch on the wall next to the metal door. A buzzer sounded, she opened the door, and we were inside.

On the other side of the door was a small room with metal mailboxes on one wall. Pipes and electrical wiring lined the other walls. Only dim light came from a bulb hanging by a wire from the ceiling. Concrete stairs with antique iron handrails led up to the apartments above. Like most older apartment buildings in St. Petersburg, there was no elevator. My first impression was the building was old enough Lenin, the first leader of the Soviet Union, could have lived there.

We wound our way up several flights of stairs until we reached the apartment. After Nadya opened the door, Rita greeted us. At that time, she wore her hair in a multicolored mohawk and dressed in punk style. The brightness of her hair contrasted with the gloomy weather outside. As she was hugging us, Nadya and I followed the Russian custom of taking off our boots inside the door and either wearing slippers or walking in socked feet inside. At first, that felt strange to me, but in time, it became second nature.

The same old feel shrouded the apartment's interior. Inside were three bedrooms, one for Nadya and Rita and the others for two young men in their 20s, also wearing punk clothing. Everyone shared a kitchen and a bathroom. The kitchen fixtures such as the sink and cabinets looked like something from the 1940s or 1950s in the United States. There was also an old gas-burning stove which had to be lit by a match. The bathroom was small and featured an equally old toilet. We ate breakfast while we talked and relaxed. However, the day was only beginning.

The plan was for me to have my own room until the wedding. After that, Nadya and I would live there until we could find a place together. The catch was the room Nadya found was in another apartment in a different part of the city. So, right after lunch, I grabbed my bag again, and she and I headed for the metro station. It was still cold and snowy, but at least it was daylight. We entered the metro and rode for about 15 or 20 minutes until we reached the end of one of the lines. After going up the escalator to the exit, I thought we were in another city. Instead of older structures, dozens of tall, modern-looking apartment buildings, many with stores on the bottom floor, dotted the skyline. Plenty of restaurants, bars, banks, grocery stores, and fast-food joints were also nearby.

Nadya knew where she was going, so I followed her. Before I got to Russia, she had spoken to a woman named Olga who owned a three-bedroom apartment in that neighborhood and lived there with her husband, a construction or maintenance worker. Her son, a university student, had just moved to his own apartment, and Olga advertised his former room for rent. Such arrangements are common in Russia. Nadya and I navigated icy and snow-covered sidewalks through rows of towering apartment buildings on our way to check it out.

The apartment was on the 16th floor of an 18-story white concrete and steel building. Once inside, the entrance area was much more contemporary than where Nadya and Rita were living, but the most important feature to me at that point was the building had an elevator.

Olga met us at her apartment door. She looked to be in her early or mid-40s, short, with black hair sprinkled with gray. Her son's English was passable, but she and her husband spoke next to no English. From what I could tell from Nadya's interpreting (she was the best interpreter I've ever heard), Olga and her family were Russian Baptists, and she was one of the leaders of a Russian pro-life organization. Not surprisingly, the apartment was much more modern than the one I had left. In addition to the bedrooms, there was an immaculate bathroom and a kitchen with a microwave, refrigerator, electric stove, and a table large enough for four. From the kitchen window, I looked at the street and ground below covered in a snowy blanket.

It didn't take long for Nadya to sign a lease and pay Olga for the first month's rent. Nadya then left as she had to teach English classes that evening. However, she had brought some food with her from her apartment and put it in the cabinet and refrigerator for me. I wouldn't see her again until sometime the next day.

A few minutes later, I motioned to Olga that I was going to my room. My first Russian home was an ordinary bedroom with a small storage area and a wall lined with shelves where the son kept some of his books and other belongings. Outside the window, twilight was descending, and streetlights were coming on. It was as good a time as any to unpack my bag. After finishing that, I could no longer resist sleep. I turned out the light and curled up on the bed. Not surprisingly, I immediately dozed off.

When I woke up, the room was dark except for the orange light coming from a clock radio on one of the shelves. The time read 6:30. I had slept for two hours. Twilight had turned to night. Olga, her husband, and her son chatted in the kitchen in a language I didn't understand, accompanied by the aroma of supper and the clatter of spoons and forks against plates. Lights from other apartments in other buildings shone through the window. As I lay on my back and placed my hands behind my head, I breathed deep and exhaled. For the only time in my five and a half years in Russia and India, I questioned myself: "What have you done?" "Why are you here?" "How could you be so crazy?" Before I sank further into self-doubt, I remembered why I came to Russia: so Nadya and I could magnify Christ and show love to others through our marriage, and I could use my English skills to serve others and help them see Jesus. "Lord, give me the strength to come out of my comfort zone," I prayed. My stomach growled. I could either stay in my room and starve or get out of my bubble and eat. Sometimes hunger can be a great motivator. I opened the door, left my tiny comfort zone, and joined the others in the kitchen.

As I walked through the door, they greeted me in Russian. I responded with one of the few Russian greetings I knew so far and added my customary American smile. After getting the dinner Nadya had left in the refrigerator, I sat at the table with the family. The son did most of the talking, going on about the usual subjects of college-age young men. He and his parents made me feel welcome, but I was still a long way from feeling at home.

Nadya met me at the apartment the next day, Friday, so we could accomplish our next order of business – finalizing our wedding plans. We took the metro again and arrived at what is known as Marriage Registration Palace Number 1, one of three municipal buildings in St. Petersburg where couples register to be married and have their official weddings. Once we entered the office, a clerk greeted us. Nadya had dealt with her and the two other clerks who worked there while submitting the necessary documents to allow us to be married. The woman, a middle-aged blonde, retrieved a file from a cabinet, looked through the forms inside, which included the documents I had sent from the Kansas Secretary of State's office, and said everything appeared to be in order. Nadya and I breathed a sigh of relief. The next step was to schedule our ceremony. We chose 4:30 p.m. Sunday, December 26, three weeks away. In Russia, weddings are considered to be civil, secular ceremonies. After the civil ceremony, a couple can have a religious or any other kind of ceremony, but it has no legal status.

The time before the wedding passed in a blur. For one thing, I was in St. Petersburg for about two weeks before the sun ever appeared through the clouds. The skies above St. Petersburg are often covered with heavy gray clouds from late fall to the middle of spring, and the constant overcast can negatively affect your mood. When the sun peeked out, my attitude seemed to improve. When days passed without a hint of sunlight, my mood darkened. More importantly, I was still acclimating myself to my new surroundings. Nadya took me shopping to buy some warm clothes and sturdy boots, but I was on sensory overload. Moving from a predominantly rural area to a large city was a significant enough change, but the fact that the big city was in a new country filled with people with different customs and speaking another language added to the adventure. An example was the first time I ever ordered lunch alone. I had finished the morning class I was teaching at a company that manufactures navigational equipment for ships. As I exited my metro station to walk to the apartment, my stomach reminded me it was after noon. One of the most brilliant ideas St. Petersburg entrepreneurs ever had was setting up mini restaurants in kiosks outside metro stations. On that day, I passed one that sold baked goods and, in the window, saw some *sosiskye testye*, literally "sausage dough," but we would call them "sausage rolls." For a few seconds, I practiced what I would say before stepping to the window and giving my order to the woman working inside. She was friendly and nicely corrected one of the many Russian grammatical errors I made throughout my time in Russia. Even better, I got what

I asked for. Any time I ordered food, I considered it a victory whenever I got anything close to what I wanted.

Some of us English teachers in St. Petersburg commiserated once about communicating in Russian, and one of the teachers offered a brilliant insight. "We shouldn't worry about it too much," he said. "Store owners don't care about our grammar or pronunciation. They just want our money." Since returning to the U.S., I have used that line numerous times to give learners confidence in speaking English in public.

The wedding day finally came. The morning was clear and cold, so I prepared by putting on a pair of warm thermal underwear under my thin trousers. After that, I traveled by metro to Rita and Nadya's apartment, where Rita used her cosmetology training to do all sorts of things to her mother's hair. Taking photos of the whole process was an English teacher colleague and friend of Nadya's named Luba, a talented photographer who also married an American the following year. After Nadya and Rita finished all the hair and makeup, we took a taxi to the marriage palace.

Up until this point, everything that happened would have been normal before any typical American wedding. That was about to change. We arrived at the marriage palace about a half-hour before our ceremony was to begin. The winter sun was setting, and the cloudless sky meant a frosty night. Across from the marriage palace lay the frozen Neva River and old, stately governmental and office buildings illuminated by streetlights and the lingering rays of twilight. As Luba took photos of every movement, we entered the building for the wedding.

With more time to look inside than when Nadya and I set our wedding date, I realized the interior of Marriage Registration Palace Number 1 indeed resembled a palace. After Nadya exchanged her winter boots for high heels, we walked up a marble staircase flanked by ornate railings and statues with a large crystal chandelier hanging from the ceiling. Behind us trailed Rita and many of our friends. At the top of the staircase was a large room where wedding parties could wait for their ceremony. This room would have fit nicely in any tsarist-era palace, with plush red carpet, sturdy and expensive-looking tables and chairs, large vertical windows, and ornate mirrors. Overlooking everything were several more crystal chandeliers and a ceiling carved with various kinds of artwork.

In the nearly four weeks I had been in the country, I already faced many new experiences, so I don't remember being especially nervous at this point. Nadya, in her blue dress, checked her hair and makeup in one of the mirrors, but she was already as beautiful as humanly possible. As the time approached for our ceremony, the people for the wedding after ours began to arrive. The looks on their faces when they saw Rita with her rainbow-colored spiked hair and some of her punk companions were priceless.

Soon, a man opened a pair of large white doors to an adjoining room, and the bride, groom, and guests for the wedding before ours left. A few minutes later, it was game time. We entered through the doorway to the arena, a spacious room as formal as the waiting area. There was no organ playing "Here Comes the Bride;" instead, some recorded classical music was piped in. Already seated were the guests. In addition to Rita's punk group, many of them were friends who attended our church, where we planned a ceremony and reception afterward. The front of the room was flanked by a Russian flag with its white, blue, and red stripes on one side and a St. Petersburg city flag of two anchors centered by a scepter on a red field on the other. Standing about halfway between the flags was a short, not fat but not skinny, middle-aged woman with wavy brown hair and black-rimmed glasses perched on the end of her nose. She officiated the whole thing.

Nadya already told me there would be no interpreter allowed, so everything would be in Russian. As I stood holding Nadya's hand, a thought came to mind that remained with me for the entire time I lived in Russia: I felt like the visiting team in the white jerseys at a football game. That was fine, but the catch was all the officials were from the Russian league, so my chances of getting any close calls were slim. As a result, my main strategy was to fly under the radar, try to blend in as much as possible, and not do anything to arouse any notice, much less suspicion.

The woman smiled and talked in a friendly yet annoyingly comical sing-song voice. I had already picked up enough Russian in my time in St. Petersburg to realize it sounded like she was giving us the same kind of advice you would hear on Oprah. The only thing I knew for certain was when she asked me anything, I was supposed to answer, "*Da*." After the woman's monologue, Nadya and I exchanged rings before we came to the central feature of the entire event: signing the wedding license. An afterthought in American weddings, the document signing was the central part of the Russian civil ceremony. After Nadya and I put our signatures where we were supposed to, the woman spoke for a few more minutes.

Suddenly, she stopped talking, and the ceremony was over. While Nadya and her women friends were hugging, I asked my new friend Larry, a tall Oklahoman and part of two Southern Baptist International Mission Board families attending our church, "What did I just agree to?"

Larry grinned and answered, "Nothing you need to worry about."

The next play in the game plan was to get in cars and drive to our church for a Christian ceremony and reception. However, as we left the room, we learned our entire wedding was under review from upstairs. One of the three women working in the marriage registration office stormed up to Nadya, holding a folder containing my documents the Kansas Secretary of State's office had sent from Topeka. The woman told Nadya the office should not have accepted my papers because the pages were stapled instead of stitched together, the standard Russian procedure.

"Someone could undo the staple and replace one of the pages," she said. To this day, I don't understand why anybody would do that. Some Russian friends later said stitching pages was a common security practice started in Soviet times, if not before. They noted that stitches were considered a more secure way to prevent forgeries or fake documents from being inserted into folders than staples.

Nadya never backed down from an argument. Her voice intensified as she replied that when we were there a few weeks earlier, the woman in the office said the documents were approved. Nadya also said the woman checked our passports to establish our identity.

"I wouldn't have approved them," the angry bureaucrat said with a sneer. "Americans never do anything right." She scampered away.

"So, are we married or not?" I asked Nadya. She nodded; we were. Later, she told me whenever she visited the marriage registration office, she had seen stacks of documents from Americans applying to marry Russians. All were stapled. She also said each of the women gave her conflicting information about what documents were required. Looking back, I won at least one close call from the Russian officiating crew, but I will never know how close a simple piece of office supplies came to derailing the wedding.

Everyone descended the staircase and got into waiting cars. By this time, it was dark, and the temperature was falling. We drove the five or 10 minutes over snow-packed and icy streets to the church. In Russia, only a few older, established Protestant churches have their own buildings. Many evangelical congregations instead meet in homes or apartments renovated into churches. For one reason, property costs are exorbitant. The other reason is the Russian Orthodox Church sometimes uses its close ties to the government to restrict evangelical activities. Our church was one of those inside an apartment building. Nadya and I had expected only a simple ceremony followed by a few refreshments, but when we walked inside, we were astounded. Our friends had decorated the walls with blue and white drapes lined with flowers and set out tables straining under tons of food.

Following dinner, the pastor, Vitaly, a native Ukrainian fluent in both Russian and English, performed the ceremony much like any North American Protestant wedding. Next came two hours of music and games. That evening, I thought that part of the wedding was taking much too long, but after attending other Russian weddings, I found out two hours was short for the reception. The only game I remember was when I had to sit blindfolded in a chair while women walked past me and touched my hand. I had to identify which hand belonged to Nadya. Fortunately, I guessed right.

A few days later, Nadya and I took a wedding trip by train to her mother Nina's home in Petrovsky, a town of 13,000 in the Krasnodar region of southern Russia. The 1,200-mile journey through snowy forests of birch trees, past villages with wooden houses and dome-capped Orthodox churches, and across frozen rivers took 40 hours, but fortunately, we didn't need to change trains. After we headed south past Moscow deeper into Russia, I began to think how fortunate I was to see places that would have been off-limits to westerners not too many years before. Even farther south, the cold relented, and the snow disappeared, replaced by rolling fields of black mud that would be covered in wheat, corn, and other crops in the summer.

Our stop was the small railway station in the city of Krymsk, where Nadya's sister and brother-in-law lived. Following a brief visit, we crammed into their tiny Zhiguli, one of the crowning achievements of Russian automotive technology, for the hour-long drive to Petrovsky. Soon, we arrived at the apartment building where Nadya's mother, Nina, lived, a four-story brick structure probably built in the 1960s or 1970s that exhibited all the lack of ostentation any true socialist architect would have desired. After we walked up the concrete stairs to the apartment, Nina greeted us. She was in her 60s, short and plump, with wavy white hair. She spoke no English. For now, she acted friendly enough to me. In fact, her favorite phrase was, *"Garold, yesh!"* ("Harold, eat!") The apartment featured a living room with an old-fashioned television set connected to a DVD player, a small, enclosed balcony, a bedroom, a bathroom, and a medium-sized kitchen. Hanging on one wall was a rug, which I learned is common in many Russian homes.

One afternoon while Nadya and her mother were doing something in the apartment, I explored the town on foot. Compared to the big cities of Moscow or St. Petersburg, the slow pace of life in Petrovsky was a welcome change. Founded in the 1800s as a Cossack village, Petrovsky, like most small towns I saw in Russia, seemed to be a mixture of Mayberry and Anatevka, the village in *Fiddler on the Roof*. Some of the neighbors kept goats and chickens, dogs ran free, and hardly any traffic moved on the streets. Most of the streets were paved, while others were dirt paths that became rutted and muddy with winter rain and snow. Plenty of other Soviet-style apartment buildings were scattered around town, but one part of Petrovsky also had many older houses with ornate woodwork and windows. Often, there was space in the rear of the homes for gardens.

I followed the sign to downtown and walked through a park. As I exited it, I stopped to examine a statue of Lenin, then passed city hall, the police station, and several stores and cafes. On the main street, there was a market area with shops inside tents where shoppers could buy anything from hats and gloves to jewelry to electronics. I finished my alone time looking at a memorial honoring Soviet military veterans from that area who served in World War II and a marker commemorating collectivization, the policy the Soviet government began in the 1920s and 1930s under Joseph Stalin, Soviet leader from 1924 until his death in 1953, which forced landowners to surrender their small farms and live on large collective farms. Confiscation of food and equipment was blamed for having a role in the famines of the 1930s when millions of people in southern Russia and Ukraine died. Resisters were arrested or sent to prison camps. Walking around town on that peaceful afternoon, I had a hard time imagining the suffering and turmoil those people endured.

Our few days away from urban life ended, however, and we took the train back to St. Petersburg. Sitting in our platzkart, Nadya said while I was on my walk, her mother criticized me, mainly for my two big sins of being an American and not being Orthodox. Nadya told her to stop badmouthing me as I was now her husband. I shrugged it off. With the wedding and New Year's holiday over, it was time for me to go to work.

# 4

# A NEW TEACHER AND A NEW HUSBAND

Soon after we got off the train from southern Russia, conflict developed between Nadya and Olga. Nadya and I began moving her things into the apartment before the wedding, but tensions flared once everything was in our room and we were living there as a couple. Most of the conflict focused on the kitchen. Among Olga's list of rules was that no food cooking in the microwave should make a popping sound, and warm food must not be placed in the refrigerator. She thought the difference in temperature between the food and the refrigerator's interior would damage the appliance's cooling system. Many other no-no's existed for not only the kitchen but also the rest of the apartment. Nadya often expressed her frustration to me in private. I supported her as much as possible, as I agreed that many of the rules were petty. Yet, Olga owned the apartment, and not much hope existed she would loosen her unwritten regulations.

I received an equally warm welcome from some of the other building residents. On three or four mornings, I got in the elevator at the same time as a tall, thin man with dark hair and glasses who looked to be in his 30s or 40s. Whenever we shared the elevator, he spoke to me with derision in his voice. The only word I understood was *"amerikanets"* ("American"), which he said in a mocking, sarcastic tone. Anyone else in the elevator also gave me a condescending look. I said nothing after the first time, but I told Nadya and Olga when it happened again. Olga said when she informed other residents that Nadya and I were moving in, many of them told her they didn't want a foreigner living there, especially an American. In my mind, I reviewed what happened to see if I was overreacting, but I didn't think so. I wished Nadya could have met the man to see what his problem was, but they were never in the elevator at the same time. Still, I felt helpless that I couldn't speak Russian well enough yet to stand up for myself. Coming just a few weeks after the grocery store cashier tossed change at me, the elevator incidents didn't help my confidence in living in a new country.

My life moved more smoothly away from the apartment, especially regarding work. With my TEFL certification combined with my journalism degree and 25 years of experience as a reporter and editor, I easily found schools wanting me to teach for them. As a native speaker, I ended up teaching mainly adults, either in classes or one on one, who could speak English at a level ranging from just past elementary to advanced. The rationale was Russian teachers, such as Nadya, could explain basic English grammar in the students' native language more easily, while native English speakers could concentrate more on speaking, especially pronunciation and vocabulary. The motivation for many adults was money. Companies, especially those doing business internationally, often contracted with language schools to conduct English classes for employees. In turn, workers proficient in English earned more pay. Similarly, native English-speaking teachers usually earned roughly twice more than native Russian-speaking instructors. For Nadya and me, no competition was involved. All our income went into the same account.

Not long after I signed a contract with my first language school in the middle of January, I was assigned to teach classes at a business. First, I was to meet with a manager at the company's office to determine a time and date when classes could begin. When I reached the closest metro station to the office building, snow outside was coming down like a blizzard. That winter turned out to be one of the worst in recent memory for St. Petersburg. Huge icicles resembling stalactites dangled from the tops of many buildings. The city placed yellow tape on the sidewalks underneath them to keep pedestrians away. Even with the precautions, several people were killed when the icy daggers plummeted on them. Workers could often be seen shoveling snow off rooftops to keep them from collapsing.

As soon as I exited the station, tiny ice pellets stung my face. The biting wind from the Gulf of Finland knifed through everything I was wearing. My boots sank deeper into the snow accumulating on the sidewalk. Finally, I reached the correct address. Once inside, I put my gloves and hat inside my coat pockets and stomped on a rubber mat to knock the snow off my boots. I next took a few steps across the lobby to the receptionist's desk, where I introduced myself and told her why I was there.

The receptionist spoke to me in English, but what she said made me pause: "You can take off your clothes there," she told me, pointing toward a hat rack across the room. I wanted to reply, "I'll take off my coat, but I think I'll keep the rest of my clothes on," but I chose to keep quiet. Still, I stored the sentence in my memory in case I needed to use it in a future lesson on what not to say to a native English speaker in a business lobby.

While I taught a few classes and individual students in my early days in St. Petersburg, I was often called on to lead what language schools called "conversation clubs." Usually conducted in the evenings after work or school, these gave learners a chance to practice their speaking skills in a non-stressful environment. I quickly found out that most English classes in Russian schools focused on grammar and translation, with little or no instruction in pronunciation or vocabulary. As a result, many of my adult students who had taken English from elementary school through university could easily answer questions on a grammar worksheet but could barely hold a five-minute conversation in English.

Almost always, schools chose bland topics for the group discussions, such as travel, favorite films, or career or education goals. For me, it was low-paying but easy work that required little or no preparation and gained me experience dealing with learners of all levels. All I had to do was listen closely, keep a curious mind, and think of good follow-up questions to maintain the conversation. Much more important to me, however, I got my initial glimpses at the culture where I was now living.

During one of the first conversation clubs I led, a 20-something woman somehow interjected the common Russian proverb, "A thief is not a thief unless he is caught," into the conversation. I had never heard it before, and it sounded foreign to a traditional Western way of looking at things. It was also more interesting than the original topic, so I decided to probe for comments while helping her and others in the group gain confidence in sharing their ideas in English.

"So, if someone steals something from your neighbor and is never caught, that person isn't a thief?" I asked her.

"Of course."

"What if that person steals something from you?"

She giggled and shrugged. The ten or so others in the group shared her opinion. That led to deeper questions when I asked participants about objective truth and absolute right or wrong. At first, they were reluctant to answer. The blank stares and faces turned toward the floor made it appear to me they had never been asked to question what they had always heard. Eventually, a few of them said they thought such ideas as truth and universal morality were outdated and not applicable to the modern world. As a teacher employed by a private business, I could say no more. I later researched online, and some Russian websites said the expression corresponded to the English, "Innocent until proven guilty." That didn't match the context of when I heard people say it, so I asked a couple of Russian friends who said the meaning was closer to, "A thief isn't a thief unless he's caught red-handed." I saw pieces of that philosophy throughout my stay in Russia, where the person who can find a way to skirt the rules is considered "clever." As one friend told me, "In the West, laws exist to help society run more smoothly. In Russia, they are obstacles to get around."

Still, that night I hoped the discussion encouraged someone in the group to think instead of only regurgitating what they heard from someone else. When I returned to the apartment later that night, I told Nadya what had happened. Her reaction was, "Just wait. The longer you stay here, the more you'll hear."

Nadya was right. What I was encountering that first winter in Russia were the initial hints of culture shock. Back in college, I experienced some culture shock moving from Georgia to suburban Kansas City, but not on this scale. Besides language, almost everything else was new, even operating toilets by pressing a button on top instead of pushing down on a handle on the side. It felt exciting to be stretched in so many ways and to see and do things I had only imagined before. Even my first weekend in St. Petersburg, visiting the Winter Palace in the distance through freezing fog and watching a fisherman drill a hole through the thick ice on the Neva River, made me pinch myself through my thick gloves to make sure it was all real. Experts call this first stage of culture shock the honeymoon phase. In this phase, everything is positive and appealing. Some people remain in this stage and end up idealizing the host culture—I never reached that point. Although, I observed and experienced many positive aspects of Russian society in my first few months in the country, especially hospitality, the close family life of many I knew, and Russia's rich legacy in art, literature, and music. I even gave the Russian government in that winter of 2010-2011 the benefit of the doubt, although that would change.

It didn't take Nadya long to challenge me on one of those positive aspects. She explained the rules of Russian etiquette call for guests to bring some small gift when invited to someone's home. Depending on the occasion, it could be chocolate, some other food or drink, or flowers. Perhaps that is the reason Russia ranked as the world's fifth-largest flower-importing nation in 2017. Therefore, it became customary to stop at either a grocery store or flower shop on the way to a friend's apartment. I told Nadya Americans rarely do that because if someone brings a gift to your house, you feel obligated to buy something when you visit them. The fancy word for it could be "reciprocity."

"That's stupid," was Nadya's exact reply. Like she was in many things, she was probably right.

Though she was Russian, Nadya experienced her own culture shock in St. Petersburg. Even if they weren't alive at the time, many St. Petersburg residents share pride from being descendants of the generation that survived the 28-month German siege of the city, then known as Leningrad, during World War II. More than 1 million civilians died in what Russians call the *blokada* ("blockade"). They also proudly proclaim St. Petersburg as the "Cultural Capital of Russia" for the city's museums, art galleries, concerts, modern dance and classical ballet, theater, and distinctive architecture. Such world-famous composers and authors as Tchaikovsky and Dostoevsky once lived there. Nadya and some of her friends who weren't born in St. Petersburg reported, however, they occasionally had to endure condescending remarks from a few overzealous Cultural Capital natives. For example, Nadya once told me a couple of older people criticized her for an innocent comment she made in a grocery store that they took as critical of St. Petersburg.

"You're not from here, so of course you can't understand," a *babushka* said.

From the beginning of my time in Russia, Nadya was my rock, especially in the first few months after the wedding when I depended on her for almost everything. With our work schedules, however, we didn't have a lot of time together. Whenever her classes finished later than mine, I made my way to the metro station and waited for her. After she got to the top of the escalator, I hesitated a second to take in her smile, and then we walked home together so we could have at least a few minutes alone before reaching Olga's apartment.

Our escape from culture shock and big-city life was our church and each other. Sunday morning was the only time we could count on not having classes, so we took advantage of it. We rode the metro a few stops down the line to the station outside Petrovsky Stadium, at the time home of FC Zenit ("Zenith"), the local professional football (soccer) club. The team now plays in a magnificent billion-dollar stadium in another part of the city, but then the compact 21,000-seat stadium was home. On game days, fans clad in sky blue Zenit jerseys with Zenit scarves around their necks crammed the escalators, while beer and vodka bottles littered the grounds outside the station, win or lose.

Instead of taking the exit leading toward the stadium, we took another exit across a small park and past a large, white Russian Orthodox church topped by golden domes with Orthodox crosses. As church bells chimed, the building was surrounded by *babushkas* kneeling and praying and sometimes selling miniature icons and other religious paraphernalia. We followed the sidewalk another couple of blocks past apartments, a bakery, a bank, and other businesses until we arrived at the apartment complex where our church, *Tserkov Novaya Zhizn* ("New Life Church"), met.

Nadya and I had faced hurt and disillusionment in some of our previous church and ministry involvement. For so long, we heard ideas met with such responses as, "How much is this going to cost?" or "We've never done it that way before." We observed people treated as spiritual projects instead of as individuals or church leaders outright lying to people. Before we were married, we often talked online about starting a "Loving Church," where we could concentrate on loving God and loving people while following Jesus and leading others to him, free from the trappings of extrabiblical legalism. Nadya found the New Life Church between the time she moved to St. Petersburg and I arrived. As she described it over Skype, it was evangelical non-denominational, although doctrine and style were strongly Baptist.

Vitaly, who conducted our Christian wedding ceremony, served as pastor. He and his wife, Alexandra, had three daughters. Two Southern Baptist Convention International Mission Board families from the U.S. also attended. Clint and his wife, Janet, were native Texans and IMB team leaders for St. Petersburg, who had two daughters and an adopted Russian son. The other couple was Larry, the Oklahoman who assured me my wedding vows in Russian were nothing to worry about, and his wife, Josie. Josie, a Philippines native, and Nadya grew closer than friends over the next few years. Thanks to these and other people in this church, Nadya and I healed from a bit of the pain and frustration of our past ministry involvement.

For me, the best way to deal with stress and culture shock was time with Nadya. Her unconditional love and acceptance, her deep, dark eyes, a smile that could brighten the darkest mood, a heart that was softer than her grin all came to the surface in our first months together. If I was ever tempted to quit in the face of life outside the comfort zone, I thought about those things. "You are the best," she sometimes told me. "And you must remember it."

One positive result of our long-distance relationship was we communicated very well. Any subject, silly or serious, was fair game. We could spend hours talking and still wish we had time for more. On the other hand, the disadvantage of living on two separate continents was if you added the week in Ukraine with the three-plus weeks after I arrived in Russia, we had spent only a month together before the wedding day. While other couples were going to movies, eating out at restaurants, or taking hikes together, we met online. This transition time was probably more of an adjustment for me as I was the one in a new culture, but it took a few weeks for us to get used to each other. Non-verbal characteristics and habits other couples detect about the other person during the dating phase were practically unknown to us until either right before or right after the wedding.

We solved the situation with good communication and prayer. After a long week of classes, one Sunday afternoon around this time in late winter or early spring 2011, Nadya and I were taking a nap. When we woke up, I was holding her close in my arms. Out of nowhere, a thought entered my mind. "Heaven must be an amazing place," I said.

"Why?" Nadya asked.

"They say Heaven is greater than anything on earth, but I can't think of anything nicer than this."

She lifted her head and kissed me gently on the cheek.

Unfortunately, the situation with Olga and the apartment didn't improve. Even some of her neighbors were upset with her. One early morning when I was up before anyone else, I opened the apartment door to leave for class. As always, I closed the door behind me, but I happened to look down at my feet. A black hairball was resting in the hallway near the door. It was larger than any hairball I had ever seen, and it looked to be intricately sewn together. Nevertheless, my immediate reaction was, "Someone needs to sweep around here."

When I returned to the apartment that afternoon, Nadya asked if I had seen the hairball. I said I had but didn't think anything of it. She told me she and Olga's son had seen it later that morning and both thought the same thing: in Russian folklore, witches sometimes use such hairballs to cast hexes or spells on someone. In this case, perhaps a resident in the building involved in witchcraft was casting a spell on Olga.

I believed Nadya, but I said this was something far removed from anything I had ever dealt with before. The hairball didn't influence our opinion, but we decided to look for a new place to live. A few weeks later, Nadya found us another apartment across town. For me, the number of new experiences—and my culture shock— were about to increase beyond anything I could have imagined.

# 5

# CONFRONTING CULTURE

Not long after we moved to our new apartment, Nadya and I attended a St. Petersburg Philharmonic Orchestra concert one early-spring Sunday afternoon at the orchestra's Grand Hall. Located near the heart of the main St. Petersburg historic district, the building resembled a palace from the outside and even more so inside. The large hall where the concert took place was exquisite — an immaculately arranged stage, white marble columns standing along the sides guarding two or three levels of balconies where boxes with luxurious red-velvet chairs were nestled, and gigantic crystal chandeliers hanging from an intricately crafted ceiling.

The performance began as all Russian concerts I saw started. A slightly overweight, middle-aged woman who looked and sounded like the person presiding over our wedding — wavy brown hair with glasses perched at the tip of her nose and the same sing-song voice — walked out on stage and talked and talked and talked, seemingly about the history of music since Babylonian times. However, once the concert opened, all that was forgotten. Even from where Nadya and I sat in the "cheap seats," not unlike the outfield bleachers at a baseball stadium, the orchestra's technique and sound were amazing, and the auditorium's acoustics ranked as the best I had ever heard.

Toward the end of the last piece, however, a distraction happened in our small corner of the concert hall. Nadya reached inside her purse for something and accidentally hit the alarm button on her cell phone. For no more than a second, the screeching sound from Nadya's phone clashed against the intricate melodies from the musicians. People around us glared, and a little old lady sitting behind us spat out words I couldn't understand. Fortunately, within two seconds, Nadya muted her phone.

After the concert ended, Nadya and I walked down the sidewalk when I asked her what the woman behind us said.

"Nothing," Nadya replied.

"No, I heard her say something," I answered. "I want to know."

"She said, 'You stupid idiot!'"

We stopped in the middle of the path as others leaving the concert walked around us. Every instinct inside me cried out to protect my wife. "Why didn't you tell me before we left? I would've said something to her."

Nadya took my hand, and we resumed walking. "Forget about it," she told me. "You'll get used to it here."

I never totally got used to it, but this incident represented the positive and negative extremes and everything in between I experienced and observed in St. Petersburg culture.

A couple of weeks before the concert, Nadya found a three-bedroom apartment in the southwestern part of town we could sublease to help pay the rent. Our arrangement was unique. The apartment owner was a middle-aged woman whose son normally lived there. However, he was in jail for the time being, though we never learned what crime he supposedly committed. The woman said he would be in prison for a while yet, and we would have to find another apartment once he was released. She added he was not the best housekeeper, so there would be lots of cleaning to do. For Nadya and me, at least we would have a place to live where our food could pop in the microwave, and we wouldn't find any hairballs outside our door.

We arranged for a truck and driver to take us and our belongings to the new apartment. Our route passed the Narva Gate, an arch dedicated in 1834 to commemorate Russia's victory over Napoleon, and a monument to Sergei Kirov, Leningrad Communist Party leader from 1926 until his assassination in December 1934. Soviet leader Joseph Stalin considered the popular Kirov a political rival but used his death as a pretext to launch the Great Purge, Stalin's brutal campaign to eliminate dissenting members of the Communist Party and anyone else he considered a threat. Estimates say at least 750,000 were executed and at least 1 million more sent to labor camps known as gulags.

By now, we left our previous concrete-and-steel, suburban-like area and entered a traditionally working-class district. The glitz from the shops, restaurants, and modern apartment buildings was replaced by older apartments and neighborhood stores that seemed to possess more character. Away from the main tourist and business zones, it's a part of the city most foreigners never see.

In about half an hour, we arrived at our new home. The apartment building was one of many "Khrushchev buildings" dotting the area. Khrushchev buildings were named after Nikita Khrushchev, Soviet leader when they were built in the 1950s and 1960s, but best known to Americans for his part in the Cuban missile crisis and for supposedly banging his shoe on a table at the United Nations. Each box-shaped Khrushchev building features a simple arrangement of four or five floors of communal-style apartments, but with only concrete stairs, no decadent Western elevators. Sometimes the light bulb over the staircase works, sometimes it doesn't. Probably thousands of Khrushchev buildings remain throughout Russia.

Nadya and I lived on the top floor of a four-story red brick building. Inside, in addition to three small bedrooms and a cramped bathroom with a shower, everyone shared a small kitchen. The kitchen contained a 1960s- or 1970s-era gas stove, an aging refrigerator, a sink, a few small cabinets, and a countertop with storage space underneath. A small, white wooden table surrounded by four rickety chairs sat in the center of the room. The remaining room was a living room with a sofa that could fold out into a bed, a recliner, and a black bookcase with glass doors protecting a library of old books. Aging wallpaper that probably began fading years earlier, and several old photos and paintings covered the walls.

Even before our move, Nadya received replies to an ad she placed looking for roommates. Soon, we had seven more people sharing our apartment—and the rent—with us: a woman university student from Russia, a male Russian and a male Nigerian university student, and an ornithologist from The Gambia who was in Russia to research birds for his doctoral dissertation. A little later, we answered an emergency ad from a young family needing a place to stay. The husband was a medical student from Zambia, while the wife came from Peru. They had a toddler-age daughter still in diapers. The family slept in the living room behind a curtain we improvised from a couple of large bedsheets.

In total, residents from six countries squeezed into the apartment. Communication between us was in Russian or English. Zhenya, the male student from Russia, could only speak a little English, and I had about the same level of Russian. In fact, the little girl was the only one in the apartment who spoke less Russian than I could at that point. If anyone needed any translation, Nadya handled it.

Our miniature U.N. had few problems, and none of them resulted from race, religion, nationality, or any of the other normal instigators for disagreements. The only roommate who caused headaches was the student from Nigeria. First, he was consistently late paying the rent, blaming the delay on missing funds from the Nigerian government. During my work-study job at the University of Kansas, I often heard Nigerian students give the same reason for the late payment of tuition or fees. Second, he violated a rule we all agreed to stipulating none of us could invite a guest into the apartment without telling the other residents in advance, especially when nobody else was home. This rule was meant to give everyone time to make sure they stored their valuables securely. No tears were shed when he found another place to live a few months later.

If Nadya and I had to name a favorite among our roommates, it would have been Pa, the ornithologist from The Gambia, a tiny West African country on the North Atlantic coast surrounded on three sides by Senegal. Short and slender physically, Pa was nevertheless tall in intelligence and kindness. He was fluent in both English and Russian and told us about many of his adventures floating down the Gambia River in search of various bird species. Especially moving was when he told about his trip to Fort James, established on an island in the river now known as Kunta Kinteh Island (formerly James Island and St. Andrew's Island). From here, throughout the 17th and 18th centuries, about 5,000 enslaved Africans a year were shipped across the Atlantic to the Americas aboard crowded, filthy, disease-ridden slave ships. Many of those who survived the crossing ended up working in silver mines in Mexico or on sugar plantations in the Caribbean, although other ships unloaded their human cargo in what became the United States. The fort and two other associated sites nearby are now listed as UNESCO World Heritage Sites.

Like roughly 90 percent of Gambians, Pa was Sunni Muslim. Despite the negative stereotypes many Americans hold for Muslims, Nadya and I got along very well with him and could speak openly with him about any subject, including religion. Pa told us he had heard the Christian gospel from African Christians, and although there were parts he could not accept, he respected our beliefs. We felt the same about him. In time, we went our separate ways, but he still occasionally crosses my mind — I should pray for him more.

Outside, winter was turning to spring. Warmer temperatures meant melting slush, lake-sized puddles covering sidewalks and streets, and mud. The change in seasons also gave me a chance to explore the neighborhood and city and meet people outside my English-teaching circle. In front of our building were a few park benches where residents from ours and nearby buildings gathered to drink, smoke, and talk. The sounds of gossip and laughter sometimes started in the early morning, died down in the late morning and afternoon, and resumed in the evening. On warm nights, it continued until close to midnight. Often, flattened cigarette butts and empty beer and vodka bottles on the ground the next morning gave evidence of their good time. Across the sidewalk from our building was a small park with a slide, merry-go-round, and other playground equipment.

One resident of our building somehow grew attached to me. I asked him his name, but he never answered. In fact, he rarely answered any question I asked. Instead, he appeared to be seeking someone to listen. The man was probably in his 50s or 60s, medium height and weight, with a face etched with wrinkles carved from years of smoking, drinking, and hard work. Only a few teeth remained in his mouth, and his breath perpetually smelled of alcohol. Almost every time I saw him, a cigarette was nestled between his fingers, or his hand was clutching a beer can. Yet, whenever he saw me leaving or entering the building, he smiled and started a conversation. He didn't know a word of English, and his slurred speech made it hard for me to understand him. I tried to speak to him the best my limited Russian would allow. I never felt any danger from him, however, and he never begged for money. Maybe he just needed a friend.

Our apartment was in a convenient location. If you walked in one direction, you would take a sidewalk past several other apartment buildings, go down a hill, walk across the major street we took when we moved, step across tram tracks, then navigate across a technical school campus before reaching your destination: "Carousel," a large grocery store that Americans would call a "supermarket." I liked Carousel a lot but didn't shop there often because it was a long way from the apartment, especially when carrying lots of heavy bags.

If you walked in the opposite direction, you would pass more apartment buildings before reaching a row of trees and a small algae-filled pond. Residents sometimes swam there in warm weather. Farther on, more park benches and trash cans usually overflowing with liquor bottles or food wrappers lined the path. Next, a pedestrian underpass allowed walkers to go underneath a major street. At the other side of the underpass in good weather was a line of *babushkas* and others selling flowers, produce, clothing, shoes, and other items. Sometimes musicians performed everything from folk songs to classical music to pop standards. After that came a line of shops and restaurants, including a Subway, which led to our metro station. It was about a 15-minute walk from the apartment to the station entrance. From there, Nadya and I explored St. Petersburg together whenever we had free time.

Almost immediately, I began to view St. Petersburg as a city of contrasts. Tourists see the historical and cultural areas dating back to the time when Tsar Peter I, better known as Peter the Great, founded the city in 1703 during a war with Sweden. The first structure Peter ordered to be built was the Peter and Paul Fortress, which still stands along the Neva River as one of St. Petersburg's most notable landmarks. To drain the marshland and lay the foundations for the fortress and other parts of the new city, Peter conscripted thousands of serfs, or peasants, from across Russia as slave labor to perform the work. Some historians believe as many as 100,000 serfs died from hunger, disease, exposure, or even wolves.

From this grew the city that became Russia's "Window to Europe." European architects, engineers, scientists, and businessmen came under Peter's invitation, and now many of St. Petersburg's older buildings appear more like something visitors would find in Italy or France than in Russia. Examples are the Winter Palace, home of the tsars from 1732 to 1917, and the cathedral inside the Peter and Paul Fortress, both designed by Italian-Swiss architect Domenico Trezzini. Visitors can see many other examples walking around the main historical district or taking tour boats on the canals, which give St. Petersburg the nickname of "The Venice of the North."

Another part of Peter's Westernization plan was to expand the arts. Inside the Winter Palace is the world-famous Hermitage museum, containing art and historical treasures dating from ancient times, such as Egyptian hieroglyphics carved on clay tablets and paintings from the likes of Rembrandt. One day a month, the Hermitage offers free admission, and I got to visit twice on free admission days. Unfortunately, I only had time to barely scratch the surface on both trips.

There are many other places, such as the Russian Museum, another home to art masterpieces, and the Mariinsky Theatre, the place to be for theater, music, and ballet. Dozens of other theaters and museums also dot the city. An apartment once rented by author Fyodor Dostoevsky has been turned into a museum, and a business where I taught classes for a short time was near the apartment where he was living when he wrote his novel *Crime and Punishment*. Across the street from the last apartment building where we lived was a small park with a statue of Russian poet Alexander Pushkin. It's hard to escape art, literature, music, and history in St. Petersburg.

That is the St. Petersburg most visitors see. The other side of St. Petersburg consists of schools and universities, banks and financial institutions, internet technology companies, a major Baltic Sea port, branch offices of numerous international firms, and smaller businesses where residents go each day to study or earn a living. Those places off the tourist trail were where most of my students worked, where I conducted most of my classes, and where most of my encounters with St. Petersburg culture took place. Not the culture of literature and music, but the culture of everyday life in a city of about 5.5 million. These are a few impressions I received from life far from the tourist hangouts:

*Not long after I moved to Russia, I realized all my expectations for personal space had to disappear. Unless jammed inside a big crowd with no escape, Americans feel most comfortable where there is some distance between them and the next person unless they share a close family or other relationship.

In Russia, however, if you are standing in line at a store, you must not allow more than 1 or 2 inches between you and the person in front of you, or someone will break in line. This happened to me until I learned better. For example, one time, I was in line at a store. There were two cash registers and two lines. When the person in front of me paid for his things, he took a few seconds to leave.

During that delay, a woman from the other line jumped ahead of me before I had time to step to the register. In many countries, the clerk would have asked the woman to return to her line. In Russia, no problem. I had to become a little more assertive.

*Russian customs about smiling baffle many Americans. Along with the proverb about the thief, there is another Russian saying that goes, "Anyone who smiles without a reason is a fool." Many people I knew in Russia took that to mean, "Anyone who smiles is a fool, period." As a result, no one in Russia smiles unless they know the person they are smiling at. Especially to Americans, that appears cold and unfriendly, but in their culture, it's normal. In their way of thinking, to smile at someone you don't know is considered rude and an invasion of privacy.

In fact, Russians often say American smiles are phony because Russians insist they save their smiles for people they care about. They think it's dishonest to smile when you don't feel like it. In some ways, I think Russians have a point. "Many Americans are surface friendly," I explained to students and others. "They act like your best friend after only five minutes, but if you bring up a serious subject, they back away."

An example some Russians gave me was they didn't like it when Americans asked them, "How are you doing?" and didn't wait for an answer. If you ask a Russian how things are going, be prepared to hear everything. At first, Russians are more reserved than many Americans, but once you gain their trust, you can't shut them up.

*Russians, in general, are much blunter than Americans. The woman sitting behind Nadya at the concert is one example. Another English teacher told me about one of her friends, an Irish woman who married a Russian man. After the wedding, the newlyweds flew to Ireland to meet the wife's mother, who cooked dinner for them on their first night in the country. After the meal, she asked her new son-in-law how he liked it. "I really didn't," the man admitted.

The mother ran to her room in tears and slammed the door behind her. "Why did you say that?" the daughter asked.

"You didn't want me to lie, did you?"

I concluded Russians blurted out many things Americans would think but never say out loud. This difference was also one of the areas where the backgrounds Nadya and I brought into the marriage played a part in our relationship. Nadya told me I was so diplomatic I could cut the rough edges off any disagreement. If I had anything negative that I needed to bring up with her, according to my life spent in the southern and midwestern U.S. where politeness reigns, I tried to soften the words as much as possible. Nadya tried to do the same, but her lifetime spent in Russian culture usually came through. Her words occasionally sounded sharper, but I knew she loved me and wanted the best for me. "To live here, you must have a thick skin," she said once. She was right.

*Never show weakness. Another major theme I noticed early in my time in Russia was how power and control guided many interpersonal relationships. The worst thing anyone could do was show weakness. Again, this played a part in my and Nadya's marriage, especially in the early stages. Out of habit, I sometimes told her, "I'm sorry" if I did anything remotely wrong.

"Stop apologizing," Nadya would say. "There's no need to apologize."

Other times in those first months together, I baffled her by "turning the other cheek" when someone did something that could have offended me. From her reaction and facial expression, I gathered she had never seen much of that before. A prime example happened one late afternoon when Nadya and I were walking down a path leading from our apartment building while a woman with two dogs on a leash was approaching us from the opposite direction. When they got a few feet away from us, I stepped off the path onto the grass to let them pass.

As the woman and the dogs continued their walk, I stepped back onto the path. However, Nadya wasn't happy. "Why did you move for those dogs? You're my husband. You're better than a dog."

For a second or two, I didn't know what to say. But after that, I remembered it hadn't taken me long to figure out these cultural differences. I told her it meant nothing to me to take a couple of steps into the grass for the dogs, and I didn't mean to give the impression I had less value than a canine. Nadya calmed down, but at that point, I don't think she understood.

Nevertheless, I don't want to leave the impression that Nadya was a hard woman with no heart. The opposite was true. These were the only areas where we had to work through our cultural baggage to become a stronger couple.

For example, homeless animals to homeless people received more than only her sympathy. Sometimes when we were walking along, and she saw a dog running free, she would say, "That dog wants to go home with me. It just doesn't know it yet." Although no dogs got free room and board with us, a few stray cats did. Her standard reasoning was, "You look like you need your mother." That was until they used the bathroom in all the wrong places. A couple of years after we were married, she became a vegetarian, at least partly because of what she saw as cruel treatment of animals killed for food.

Her compassion wasn't limited to animals, however. When she lived in Nizhnevartovsk as a newly divorced woman with little income and a young daughter to care for, she let several homeless women live in her apartment until they could find jobs or escape abusive husbands. After we were married, on more than one occasion, she found warm food and places to stay for homeless persons we saw sleeping on park benches or on the sidewalk. One cold winter afternoon, we entered our apartment building, walked up the concrete stairs to our floor, and saw a wrinkled, middle-aged man with a scraggly beard, clothed in no more than rags, drowsing in a filthy green sleeping bag. Despite the fact he smelled like he hadn't showered in months, Nadya warmed up some leftovers for him and called someone she knew from a local homeless shelter to find a place for him to stay.

For me, some of these cultural differences I experienced were the beginning of the second stage of culture shock: frustration. The honeymoon period, where I looked on everything Russian as fresh and new, passed quickly. As much as I didn't want to do it, I now looked unfavorably on many things I experienced or observed in St. Petersburg, bureaucracy, long lines, pushy people; it didn't matter. Since returning to the U.S., I've told some Americans when they see immigrants say negative things about the U.S., it's not necessarily because they hate the U.S., but because they miss their own country. I was forced to encounter different ways of thinking and re-examine many basic facts I thought I knew. In short, I was taking another giant step outside my comfort zone.

Apart from my culture shock, schools and students were pleased with my teaching, and I was given more classes. One I took advantage of was teaching mainly conversation skills, usually correcting vocabulary or pronunciation or explaining idioms and expressions, to more advanced students — mostly managers — at a cigarette factory owned by the American tobacco manufacturer, the R.J. Reynolds Tobacco Company. Teachers could take a company shuttle bus at a metro station in the south part of the city and travel about 20 miles south to the factory in a small town named Izhora. It was nice to get out of the city, and the extra pay included in the job helped.

Growing up in the Cold War, I had always been curious about what was going on behind the Iron Curtain. One of my first students at the factory gave me a peek. He was a man in his 50s or early 60s who had some sort of job with the Soviet defense ministry before the collapse of the Soviet Union. His lone assignment every day was to study satellite photos of Detroit, Michigan, especially looking for likely roads to use in case of invasion or for possible escape routes. I told him I didn't want to tell the USSR government how to do its business, but someone from the Soviet embassy in Washington could have gone to a store and bought a road map for a lot less trouble and expense. The man smiled and answered, "We thought your road maps were fake like ours." He also had a friend who worked at the Soviet military attache's office in Vienna. His orders were to measure the quickest routes to get through Vienna and inform Moscow of any road construction going on in the city, even if it was only repairing a pothole.

Several students also signed up to take private lessons with me. I normally taught these at the apartment and at higher pay than I could make with a private school. Two of those students remain good friends to this day. One of them was Mikhail, who went by his anglicized name "Michael." Michael answered an online ad Nadya submitted about me on a Russian website. Michael told her he was an Internet Technology worker looking for a native-speaker teacher to help him prepare for a job interview in another month for the St. Petersburg office of a Canadian I.T. firm. The catch was that the interview was in English, and he said his English skills needed a lot of polishing.

Before his first lesson, I found articles that listed anywhere from seven to thirty common job interview questions. In addition, I used my own experience conducting job interviews as an assistant editor and managing editor for newspapers, as well as my trials and tribulations as a job applicant. Five mornings a week for almost a month, Michael showed up at our apartment for practice. His English needed lots of work, but he was a willing learner. I constantly pummeled him with questions as if I were the interviewer. For each answer, I gave a review and critique, both for grammar and content. When the time came for his interview, he called after it was over to tell me he thought he did well, but they offered him a second interview. That sounded encouraging, I said. He gave me another call following the next interview to say the company was flying him to Canada for a third interview. In the end, he got the job and thanked me profusely. He even gave me the nickname "Master Yoda," which he still calls me.

Michael then encouraged his oldest daughter, Anastasia (or "Nastya" for short in Russian), to take lessons from me. Anastasia excelled in her high school English class, but her father said the problem was she knew more than the teacher. Michael was right. He asked if I could help her with more advanced English, and, of course, I agreed. My main advice to her was to do what the instructor said in class but forget it as soon as she walked out the door. She went on to speak English at an almost native level, which was helpful because she was seeking a career in the travel industry. Like her father, she also remains a good friend.

As spring of 2011 became summer, I was confronting my reactions to my new surroundings. I passed the initial stage where I saw everything as a new arrival and my next stage where I focused on the wedding. I was now encountering people whose ideals and ways of thinking contrasted, widely sometimes, with what I was accustomed to in the U.S. No longer was television the only place where I had ever seen Russians: the times I watched military officers standing on the podium with tall hats and a chest weighed down with medals at Red Square on May Day, or Olympic athletes having gold medals draped around their necks while the Soviet national anthem played in the background. Instead, they were real humans, not caricatures formed by Cold War propaganda.

A combination of things carried me through this period. One, Nadya and I were convinced there had to be a reason why God would match someone from the middle of Kansas with someone from the middle of Siberia. All the difficulties we went through before the wedding were to prepare us for His mission to share the love of Jesus with others and, if possible, lead them into a relationship with Christ (Colossians 1:28). In addition, despite differences in backgrounds and culture, Nadya and I were growing closer in our marriage. Second, my natural curiosity spurred me to observe, learn, and understand no matter the obstacle. For me, I can't imagine life without this interest in the world around you. People, places, art, music, literature, and foods all are part of God's creation for us to enjoy. Sadly, many Christians I know have stumbled into a world of tribalism where they prefer to surround themselves with only those who think and believe the way they do. Instead of the Bible or other Christ-followers, they choose to be discipled by whoever says what they want to hear. Any statements or actions outside their preconceived notions are met with hostility. It seems like a terrible way to live.

Although I didn't realize it yet, I was only in the lower-division undergraduate course of my cross-cultural study. The upper-division undergraduate course was to come. Far ahead lay the graduate program. Next, however, God had other plans for Nadya and me. It was off to India.

# 6

# INDIA INTERLUDE, PART 1

Long before Nadya and I were married, Anatoly, the associate pastor of Nadya's church in the city of Nizhnevartovsk who I met in Ukraine, asked Nadya to teach English for his orphanage ministry in India. She was interested, and I told her I was, too. Now that the wedding was over and we were settled in St. Petersburg, Anatoly pressed her for an answer. She agreed, but the reasons were complicated.

A few years earlier, Nadya defied her ultra-Orthodox mother and accepted an invitation from a woman friend to a particular Protestant church in Nizhnevartovsk. For a Protestant church in Russia, especially Siberia, it was large, mainly because the messages and music were upbeat. Still, it turned out it the church taught the prosperity gospel — God rewards increases in faith with increases in health and wealth — and Nadya, even as a new Christian, sensed something wasn't right.

That feeling grew after she became one of the three secretaries for the pastor, Maxim. Nadya said he usually asked her to pad the attendance figures from Sunday services, lie on his resume and biographical profile, and perform other duties she considered dishonest. Maxim needed to embellish the truth because he sought to keep his reputation as one of the leading charismatic pastors in Russia. He was often interviewed for Russian Christian publications and appeared on a Russian Christian television network. In addition to notoriety, he also gained wealth. For example, he owned *dachas* (country homes) on the Black Sea and in Bulgaria and took an annual deep-sea fishing trip to Thailand. His adoring church members gave him an imported Cadillac for his and his wife's 25th wedding anniversary, and he once conducted a weekend seminar on "How to Properly Honor Your Pastor." His ministry became what Nadya called a "cult of personality."

Because of the physical and psychological pain she had experienced, Nadya wanted to help those facing domestic abuse, alcoholism, drug addiction, and other problems. She convinced Maxim to allow her to start a telephone helpline affiliated with the church and soon found volunteers to take calls. Although the helpline found assistance for many people, none of them attended or gave money to the church. As a result, after about six months, the pastor ordered the ministry stopped. Even harder for Nadya to accept was many of the upstanding church members disapproved of Rita's hairstyles, tattoos, and taste in music and let it be known with critical comments or reproving looks. Rita gave up on the church and maybe even God, at least for a while. Nadya, meanwhile, grew tired of women's meetings focusing on fashion and makeup tips instead of prayer and Bible study.

What kept Nadya at the church was the assistant pastor, Anatoly, and his wife, Maria. While Maxim gave the impression of embodying the imperial pastorship, Anatoly appeared friendly and down-to-earth. He often spoke in small native villages near Nizhnevartovsk and led mission trips to Kazakhstan and different parts of Russia. Nadya looked up to him and Maria, and they became good friends. This was about the time I met Nadya.

Maxim viewed Anatoly's popularity as a threat to his control, while Anatoly resented Maxim's dominance. A power struggle ensued. A string of verbal salvoes and backroom machinations erupted into open conflict during a Friday night seminar at the church when Maxim publicly fired Anatoly for insubordination. In a hastily called meeting following the seminar, Maxim and his carefully selected *politburo* (a.k.a. board), consisting of 12 members of the church *nomenklatura* and others in the vanguard of the church proletariat, voted unanimously to excommunicate Anatoly and his followers, including Nadya. During the Sunday service, two days later, Maxim informed the congregation of the purge and banned church members from communicating with anyone who had been expelled.

One of those kicked out was a woman named Tamara who had amassed a fortune in the lucrative Nizhnevartovsk real estate market. As a center for oil and natural gas production, Nizhnevartovsk attracted many petroleum engineers and professionals in related fields willing to pay premium prices for housing. Tamara wanted to use her wealth to open an orphanage in India and eventually add more orphanages there. After the church split was the ideal time, she thought, to offer Anatoly the job as director. Under the plan, she and members of a board of directors would be in charge of funding and overseeing operations, while Anatoly would direct the ministry in-person. With no other immediate options for employment, he accepted. He soon worked with some Indian church leaders to purchase and renovate a house in Goa, a picturesque city along the Arabian Sea on the west coast of India, to use as an orphanage.

Teaching the children English was to be one of the keys to the ministry, and Anatoly wanted Nadya to be the one to instruct them. He tried to get Nadya to India before we were even married but could not get her a visa. After the wedding, Anatoly pressured her to make a decision. While she would be the primary teacher, I would come along as her assistant. As I was in Russia to experience and observe as much as possible, I had no objections. Our church in St. Petersburg even unexpectedly gave us the money to cover our airfare. By the first of November, we had our Indian visas and were ready to go. However, a few days before we left, Anatoly told Nadya that the ministry had added another orphanage in a city named Bareilly, and they wanted us to teach there instead of Goa. All Nadya and I could learn before the trip was Bareilly was a city of nearly one million near the Nepal border in northeastern India, far from any tropical beaches. We would find out the rest later.

On an early evening in November, we left St. Petersburg aboard an Emirates Air flight. Our plane sliced through the leaden gray clouds that hang over St. Petersburg almost continually from late fall to spring and headed south for a six-hour flight to Dubai, an extravagantly wealthy oil, business, and tourism metropolis on the Persian Gulf. From there, we would change planes and fly to New Delhi, the capital and largest city of India, and meet Anatoly and Maria.

It was dark, and the clouds were long gone by the time we passed over the Persian Gulf. Soft light from a full moon reflected on the waves as three or four oil tankers sat in the water. The scene appeared peaceful compared to the turbulent political realities in the region. Soon after that, the bright lights of Dubai pierced the black desert night, and we landed. As we got off the plane, we descended steps leading to the tarmac, where we boarded a shuttle bus to the international terminal. Even after midnight in November, the temperature was 80°F. Nadya and I were already sweating underneath our warm Russian coats and clothing. I told Nadya I couldn't imagine what it would feel like there on a July afternoon.

Inside the terminal, the mixture of cultures was amazing. Westerners in shorts and tennis shoes walked next to Arabs dressed in traditional robes. Nadya and I heard probably three or four languages spoken just in the area where we were sitting. We had four hours to wait for our next flight, so I let Nadya doze off while I kept watch over our carry-on bags. After we boarded the plane to India, I fell asleep, so I don't remember much about that four-hour flight except I caught a glimpse of the white desert sands and mountains of Pakistan in the early-morning sunlight before we arrived in New Delhi.

Anatoly and Maria were waiting for us in the airport terminal. Anatoly and I loaded the bags into a small car they were renting, and away we went. Our destination was an orphanage run by a Russian Baptist missionary couple where we were staying for a few days before going to Bareilly. The missionary couple and their children were away for some reason which I can't remember. Leaving the terminal area, Anatoly drove the car onto a modern six-lane highway lined by well-manicured lawns and trees. While Maria and Nadya sat in the back seat catching up on everything (Maria's English was excellent), I tried to have a conversation with Anatoly, but his English wasn't the best, and my Russian was worse.

A few miles later, we exited the highway and entered another world. The change was abrupt. No more freeways, modern office buildings, or other trappings of 21st-century life. Instead, the narrow street we took drove us into a time warp. Traditional Indian markets selling fruit, produce, and other foods sat next to tiny shops selling tablets and cell phones. Women dressed in colorful robes called "saris" walked along the street with baskets or jars perched on their heads. Dogs, horses, and cattle roamed freely and often fed on heaps of garbage lying on the ground. Jamming the thoroughfare were cars, motor scooters, and small three-wheeled vehicles called "auto-rickshaws," which usually served as taxis. Hindi pop music coming from stores and vehicles provided the soundtrack, along with the constant accompaniment of blaring car horns.

We left the crowded market area and drove through a middle-class neighborhood with two- or three-story, flat-roofed houses surrounded by walls and gates. In about 15 minutes, we arrived at the house where we would stay for three days until we left for Bareilly.

As soon as we walked through the doorway, Anatoly and Maria introduced us to the two other volunteers accompanying us to Bareilly. The first was a middle-aged Ukrainian woman named Alexandra. She had heard Anatoly give presentations at her home church about the orphanage ministry, which inspired her to come to India. Alexandra's role would be to help with the cooking, cleaning, and laundry at the Bareilly orphanage and provide any assistance Nadya and I needed with English classes. The other volunteer was a middle-aged South African woman named Laura. She had served as a missionary in Yemen for a short time and knew Anatoly through taking a Bible correspondence course he taught. She planned to travel to Bareilly with us, stay for a few days, then proceed with Anatoly and Maria to Goa, where she would teach English at the orphanage there. She had no training or experience as a teacher. Her only qualification was she had spoken English her entire life. However, Anatoly reasoned Maria would be there to help her.

Anatoly left for a while to return the rental car. When he came back mid-afternoon, he decided he would take us on a brief tour of New Delhi, followed by a stop at an Indian restaurant for dinner. The first hurdle, negotiating the price for two auto-rickshaw drivers to transport the six of us, took a while. With that settled, Nadya, Alexandra, and I got in one and Anatoly, Maria, and Laura in the other. Making our way down a four-lane road separated by a median, we were in the middle of afternoon rush hour. Cars, trucks, motorcycles, and scooters clogged the road as exhaust fumes clogged our nasal passages. More Hindi music blasted from car radios or CD players, while Muslim prayers came from a loudspeaker at a mosque. The road was lined with dozens of small shops and markets and dingy white walls plastered with faded and torn billboards written in Hindi and English. At one point, a man and a baby elephant were sitting under a large tree.

Our vehicles coasted down a large hill where we had to stop for a red light at an intersection. In the median, a policeman clad in a spotless, immaculately pressed white uniform was directing traffic while holding a gold whistle in his white-gloved hands. The policeman wasn't alone, however. In the same median stood three young children. The first was a young girl, perhaps age 6 or 7, barefoot, wearing a threadbare blue dress. She carried an infant whom Alexandra, Nadya, and I figured was her brother or sister. The baby was shirtless but was wearing a once-white diaper that looked like it needed to be changed. The other child was a boy, perhaps age 8 or 9, wearing a plaid, button-down shirt with brown shorts and sandals. He was kicking a tin can at the edge of the street near where we stopped. All three children were thin and dirty. The cross-street traffic continued before Nadya spoke up: "Why doesn't someone stop and help? A car could hit them."

The light turned green, and the policeman signaled it was our turn to go. We looked back at the traffic speeding inches from the children, but Nadya and I didn't know what to do. In hindsight, this scene could be a composite of much of what we were to observe in Indian life: the constant, noisy bustle of people juxtaposed with the well-dressed police officer standing next to the shabbily dressed children playing in the street. At the time, however, Nadya and I could do nothing but sit in the auto-rickshaw feeling inadequate. We were overwhelmed by the fact that this symbolized a much bigger issue of the gap between poverty and wealth. It wasn't the only time India perplexed us.

From there, we passed through a wealthy neighborhood with mansions and palm trees on the way to the India Gate, an arch resembling the Arc de Triomphe in Paris unveiled in 1933 to honor Indian soldiers who died while serving in the British Indian Army during World War I and a couple of later imperial wars. We next saw the Indian Parliament building and the Indian presidential palace, where, along with Indian Army guards and weapons, we had our first glimpse of monkeys living outside of a zoo. Twilight turned to darkness as we returned to our vehicles and made our way to a Western-style shopping mall with an Indian restaurant in the food court. I don't remember what I ate, but it tasted delicious.

The next day, Nadya and I took another bumpy auto-rickshaw ride with Anatoly to have lunch and discuss our duties in Bareilly in more detail. It was late morning, but the heat and humidity already made New Delhi feel like a sauna. We arrived at one of the thousands of markets dotting the city and were greeted by the aroma of chili and garlic powder coming from food stands. Nadya and I later determined no one could adequately describe India without including the smells. As we made our way through a maze of stores, some shopkeepers tried to entice Nadya with silk cloth or carved elephant figurines. She politely declined. Anatoly led us to a restaurant lined with cafeteria-style tables and open on one side to let air and flies circulate. After sampling more Indian food, we got down to business.

Anatoly told Nadya and me he wanted us to teach English not only to the children but also to Alexandra and the Indian staff at the orphanage. Alexandra spoke no English, while the Indian workers could speak some. We understood that but what he said next caught us off guard. "In recent months, I've become more involved with ministry to Myanmar," he said, referring to the south Asian country formerly known as Burma. "It means my duties in India are almost done. I'd like to focus on Myanmar and hand over my duties here to someone else."

I asked the silly question, "Who?"

Anatoly smiled and said he wanted me to take over for him. Nadya's mouth gaped open, and I almost spit out the rice I was chewing. In my mind, I was shocked at the suggestion, but outwardly I thanked him. I added I had never even been inside an orphanage until the night before and knew nothing about running one. Anatoly nodded but said nothing. He next asked if we had any more questions about Bareilly. I wanted to know if there would be any chance to get out of the orphanage and interact with the people, as that was one reason I came.

"Most of your time will be spent teaching English," Anatoly replied. "After that, you may do anything you like. I don't want anyone sitting around bored."

Nadya told Anatoly that she and I had talked before we left Russia about having a Bible study in the orphanage at night for neighbors or others. Anatoly shook his head. "I figure we're never going to reach this generation of Indians," he said. "There is no use trying. They're lost and will never change." He continued, "The best way to reach India is through the orphans. We can get them when they're young, teach them about God, and train them to be the future Christian leaders of India. You could call it 'orphanage evangelism.'"

As I was mentally digesting Anatoly's missions strategy, I asked him if it would be necessary to learn any Hindi to communicate better with the people. He put his elbows on the table and replied, "Why sit around on your butt all day doing that when you don't need it? I've got better things to do than waste my time on something I can do without."

Nadya and I glanced at each other as Anatoly paused before speaking again. "One thing you must keep in mind," he said just above a whisper, "is the Indian people aren't very intelligent. In fact, they're a little stupid. If you tell one of them to do something, you're never certain if it will be done right or if it will be done at all." He was on a roll, so the words kept gushing. "Another thing," he said, "is you can't trust them. They'll lie, but I don't know if they lie because it's in their character or if they lie because they do anything to avoid conflict and would rather lie than face the truth. You never know where you stand with them."

Anatoly added one more thing: "We want to help the poorest of the poor. We're the only ministry that really cares about India. None of the rest does. Just us."

Nadya and I were too shocked to respond to anything he said.

That night when we were alone in our room, we reviewed our lunchtime conversation. In her eyes, I could see the disappointment in Anatoly where I had only seen admiration before. One of her many facial expressions I learned in our 11 months together so far was that when her eyes narrowed and her lips tensed, she was on the way to becoming angry. That was the look she showed me that night. Anatoly's descriptions of the Indian people appalled us, while we decided we didn't need anyone's permission to connect with people outside the orphanage.

Two days later, the six of us boarded an early-morning train to our new home in Bareilly. Crammed inside the slow-moving behemoth, people in the rear were hanging out windows and doorways while others were perched on top of the cars. The six-hour trip crossed flatlands which reminded me of the African savanna, although a thin layer of yellow dust caked on the windows made it hard to see clearly outside. Along the way, monkeys roamed the platforms at some of the stations where we stopped, ignoring the dogs that sometimes barked at them.

I was ready to stand and stretch my legs when we arrived at the Bareilly station. Anatoly and Maria had been there before, so they led the way off the train. We navigated through a maze of passengers hurrying to and from trains, vendors hawking everything from water to jewelry, and elderly men and women with creased, hardened faces squatting next to the brick building with their hands outstretched, silently begging for money or food.

Inside the station, our eyes hadn't had time to adjust from sunlight to dark when a couple of male voices came from the throng: "Brother! Sister!" Before I realized what was happening, two Indian men ran toward Anatoly and Maria, hugged them, grabbed most of our luggage, and led us outside. We crossed a gravel-covered parking area until we came to a couple of auto rickshaws. The Indian men — one tall and the other short — placed some of the bags on top of each vehicle and tied them with ropes while Anatoly and I stuffed the rest inside. In a few minutes, we were ready to go.

Alexandra, Nadya, and I rode in the auto-rickshaw driven by the taller man, who told us his name was Sandeep. He and his wife, Kavita, who we would meet later, handled the day-to-day operations of the Bareilly orphanage. The driver of the other auto-rickshaw, Paul, served as an assistant. Nadya and Sandeep did most of the talking as we chugged down the dusty street, occasionally jarred by potholes. I was in observation mode. It was Saturday afternoon — market day — and produce and vegetable markets, clothing stores, and jewelry shops were packed with people. Cars, trucks, and motor scooters spewed exhaust fumes into the hazy, humid sky as they competed for space on the street with horse-drawn wagons, cows, and dogs. Hindi music blaring from cars or speakers attached to stores provided the soundtrack. A narrow, brick-lined trench ran along one side of the street, where flies and mosquitoes hovered over the dark, brackish water. "I always wondered what an open sewer looks like," I thought. "Now I know."

After we passed more shops and markets, we reached the top of a hill. Below stood a large Catholic church and school encircled by a low brick wall with a garden and statues in front. We followed the road down the hill, passed the school, and came to a neighborhood with a mixture of homes and small shops. Many of the houses looked almost dilapidated, but the stores and markets appeared to be in better condition. In the middle of the area was a large open field where horses, donkeys, and cattle were grazing.

A little bit farther, we came to a narrow alley blocked by an iron gate. Sandeep stopped the rickshaw and got out to open the gate so we could continue. The first house on our left was a small brick structure barely tall enough for an adult man to stand upright. Gaps in the wall showed where some bricks were missing, and the yard was mostly dirt and littered with trash. The other houses we passed appeared to be more for middle-class residents, all with flat roofs and surrounded by walls and gates. Plenty of trees and shrubs lined both sides of the path. At the end of the street, we could go no farther. A yellow brick wall about 15 or 20 feet high stood ahead. The only passageway through the wall was a small door used by pedestrians and animals of various kinds to reach another business area on the other side. We parked in front of a four-story white house surrounded by a white wall, with a gate leading to a driveway and small carport. There were also the customary flat roofs. An open sewer ran in front of the house and continued all the way down the street. On one side of the house was an empty lot filled with weeds and trash. This was the orphanage.

We walked inside the house into a large, open room used for meals and morning and evening devotions. As soon as we entered, Sandeep's wife, Kavita, greeted us individually, wearing a formal, colorful sari.

After that, Sandeep introduced us to the seven smiling orphanage children. The youngest was Sumit. He was about five years old and was missing his top front teeth. Sandeep told us he was usually happy and playful, although he often tried to use his status as the youngest to his advantage. Standing next to him was Suraj, about age 7. He could be a mischievous troublemaker, but his smile and laugh covered a multitude of sins. Sandeep said he and Paul found the two boys huddled alone in the Bareilly train station one morning and took them in. Their parents had apparently put them on the train and abandoned them, presumably because they couldn't afford them. Somehow the boys ended up in Bareilly. No one knew their ages.

Next was a boy named Abhijeet, about age 8 or 9. He was born in the eastern Indian state of Orissa (as presumably, all the children were) to Christian parents who were killed by Hindu extremists during anti-Christian violence there in 2010. Although he smiled a lot, we adults wondered if he might have some sort of post-traumatic stress disorder as his mind sometimes seemed to withdraw into another world. Alongside Abhijeet stood Asmita, also age 8 or 9, the only girl in the group. Her parents died from an illness, and she was placed in the orphanage. The women loved to run their fingers through her jet-black hair.

The final three were the oldest boys. All were about 10 years old. Milan (pronounced ME-lahn) was artistic, creative, and sensitive. Everyone marveled at his artwork. Rashikant was good at numbers and problem-solving and still carried tribal markings on his face when he arrived at the orphanage. His grandfather was the first person in his tribe to convert to Christianity. Sandeep saved most of his praise, however, for the oldest, Moses. Moses' parents had been pastors but died from disease. From them, Moses inherited a deep spirituality. Often when the other children were playing, he, usually along with Milan and Rashikant, stayed in their room to pray for them. Moses also spoke many times at morning and evening devotions, where even at age 10, he could move adults with his preaching.

While Nadya and the others toured the rest of the house, I stayed on the first floor with the children. They showed me the kitchen, a storage room for food and school supplies, Sandeep and Kavita's room, and the two children's bedrooms. There was also a smaller bathroom for the kids and a larger bathroom for adults. On the wall next to the storage room were a map of India and a poster with the Hindi alphabet. Each room for the children had bunk beds, and plain blue walls displayed drawings, pictures, and schoolwork. Inside one of the rooms, Moses spoke up, "Uncle, we want to learn English." (Indian children are taught to call all adult men "uncle," and all adult women "aunty," with the accent on the "ty." In Christian circles, it's considered rude to call someone by their first name without adding "brother" or "sister" first.)

"Today is Saturday, and we'll start classes Monday," I answered with a smile.

The children insisted. They wanted an English lesson immediately. I hadn't expected such enthusiasm, so I went with the first thing that came to mind, the song, "Head and Shoulders, Knees and Toes," complete with motions, always a children's English as a Second Language favorite. Fortunately, no video evidence of this exists. After I explained some of the words and showed them the motions to go with the music, we sang it a few times. The kids sang and laughed and seemed to enjoy it. After about the third time through, Nadya and the others returned downstairs. I told Nadya the children already wanted an English lesson, so she took over and taught them "Eensy, Weensy Spider," including all the finger motions. With her smile and soft voice combined with the way she caressed the faces of some of the children, the kids fell in love with her right away.

After the impromptu singing, I toured the rest of the house myself. On the second floor were three bedrooms on one side. Nadya and I had a bathroom adjoining our room, but first, we needed a lesson on using Indian squat toilets. As the name implies, you placed your feet on grooves on the side and squatted over the bowl. Once you were done, there was a faucet next to the toilet where a small plastic bucket was provided to fill with water and "flush" everything into a septic tank. Many residents of India and other countries that use squat toilets insist they are more hygienic than Western-style toilets.

There was also a small kitchen area and a large open space leading to the second-floor roof. The roof and living area were separated by a tall iron gate with a small doorway. On the roof were clotheslines and vines where gourds grew. The children spent a lot of time there, as the house had no yard. Paul's room was on the third floor, while more storage room was on the fourth floor. A family of four monkeys also lived on the top floor. Every morning they would leave the house about 8:00 or 8:30 and return about 4:00 or 4:30 in the afternoon.

It was the middle of November, but the weather remained warm. All of us were preparing for bed that first night when we heard loud Hindi music accompanied by shouts and laughter from a crowd of people. Kavita said the music was coming over a loudspeaker from a large Hindu temple nearby, as this was the height of Hindu wedding season. About midnight, the volume came down, but on some nights, you could still hear the festivities until 2 or 3 a.m. At the other end of the spectrum, the first Muslim prayers of the day regularly came at 5:30 a.m. over a loudspeaker from a mosque in the other direction. Until Hindu wedding season was over a few weeks later, we didn't get much sleep.

English classes for the children began on Monday morning. Nadya and I brought two laptops with a hard drive, our printer, and lots of books and notebooks containing photocopies of articles and worksheets to use. Our classroom was the large room where we met the children when we arrived and ate our meals. Posters of the English alphabet and various vocabulary words, as well as a chalkboard, adorned the walls. Sandeep and Kavita had already bought the children notebooks and pencils. For this first lesson, all the adults were watching. Anatoly wanted Laura to see how it was done.

"Today, I learn English," Suraj said with his customary grin. The children could already speak some English, but they could also speak their own native tribal language and some Hindi. They were as well-behaved as children their age could be expected to be, and they seemed eager to learn. Nadya led them through some simple songs and sentences, and all was going well until she got to the alphabet. Instead of simply having the children repeat the letters of the alphabet, she taught them the sounds of each letter.

Sandeep stood and objected. "Sister, I only teach them the letters," he said in an angry tone.

Nadya remained calm. "Brother, I think it is more important that they learn correct pronunciation."

Sandeep stormed out of the room and drove off in the orphanage's tiny gray Suzuki compact car. But it was the first and the last time he ever questioned Nadya's teaching methods. Nadya was not offended, and Sandeep never mentioned it again. My suspicion was Kavita calmed him down. As would always happen in future classes, the lesson ended with a video and more songs. I thought the first lesson was a success.

That afternoon came the first English lesson for Alexandra and the Indian staff. Alexandra, who knew no English at all, didn't seem interested. Sandeep, Kavita, and Paul spoke some English, but they could never get the hang of grammar and pronunciation. Alexandra told Nadya she couldn't care less about learning English, and the others often found more pressing things to do around the orphanage. After a few weeks, we decided to stop the adult classes.

A few days later, Anatoly, Maria, and Laura left by train to the Goa orphanage, and we settled into a routine. Mornings began with the children getting out of bed and cleaning up, devotions usually led by Kavita, and breakfast. After that, we adults had breakfast, and then Nadya and I set up for English class. Math class followed English and Hindi lessons led by Sandeep. Then there was afternoon free time, evening devotions usually led by Sandeep but also sometimes by Moses and even me, dinner, and bed. That was the schedule Monday through Friday, except we had no English lessons on Saturday and Sunday.

For our meals, we sat on a large rug rolled out on the floor of the large room. Westerners could use utensils if they wished, but Indians ate with their hands unless there was soup on the menu. Lunch and dinner consisted of a mound of rice topped with different spices and vegetables and chapati, an Indian bread similar to tortillas. We only had meat on Wednesday evening, which was beef night, and Saturday night, which was chicken night. Every Saturday afternoon, Sandeep drove down the street to a store with cages of live chickens in front. He would choose a chicken, and an employee would take it inside the building and place it on a wooden table. There, the man cut off the chicken's head, drained the blood through a hole in the table into a bucket below, plucked the feathers, skinned it, chopped the meat into bite-size pieces, and placed the pieces inside a plastic bag. Two or three hours, the chicken was the main dinner ingredient. Nadya and I went to watch it several times.

Evening devotions began with singing Hindi praise and worship songs accompanied by Milan on the bongo drums. The kids enthusiastically sang with their whole hearts, and you couldn't help but smile. Sandeep and Moses usually spoke in Hindi, usually about different Bible stories at a level the children would understand. I offered to speak sometimes, and Sandeep readily accepted. My first talk was from Judges 7, where God tells Gideon his 30,000 men are too many to defeat the Midianites, and they end up with 300, which was enough to defeat the enemy. I also did a series on what the children would need to do to prepare for school and life outside their Christian "greenhouse." I explained to them that at the orphanage, we adults did everything we could to teach the children Christian values and try to prepare them for success in school and their future lives. However, once they went to school, they would encounter difficult situations where they would need to rely on the lessons taught them at the orphanage. I enjoyed it, and I think the children did, too.

Although Nadya and I felt blessed at the beginning of our time in India, it didn't take long for negatives in the ministry to pop up. One problem emerged when Laura exhibited her dissatisfaction soon after she began teaching English. In New Delhi, she announced her two primary purposes for being in India were to engage in "spiritual mapping," the technique of supposedly determining a demon's geographical area of power to do battle with it, and to rid India of what she called its 140 million idols (I have no idea how she arrived at that figure). When Laura asked Anatoly if she could do spiritual mapping after each morning's English class, Anatoly refused, saying he wanted her to focus on improving her teaching skills. The Goa children were also much more unruly than the Bareilly kids, which led to discipline problems on top of her classroom inexperience. After a week or so, the disillusioned missionary grew sullen at Anatoly's lack of interest in her spiritual quest. As soon as each day's lesson was over, she walked to the beach about a mile away and sat in the sand or on a rock until dinner time. She ate her meals alone in her room.

Within a month, Laura boarded a plane back to South Africa. She never returned.

Our most immediate concern, however, was the weather. About two weeks after Anatoly, Maria, and Laura left, temperatures in Bareilly suddenly dropped. Temperatures at night plummeted into the 40s Fahrenheit, which doesn't sound cold, but only two or three orphanage windows had glass, and there was no heating unit. As a result, the house became a freezer except for a few hours in the afternoon when the sun generated some warmth. Occasionally, we built fires in the open space on the second floor.

Nadya contacted Anatoly about the situation, but his reply was curt: "You have to be willing to suffer for the Lord."

"I'm very willing to suffer for the Lord, but in this case, it's unnecessary," she replied. "Can't you do something? We're afraid the children could get sick." She asked if Anatoly could send more warm clothes for the youngsters. He answered the money wasn't available from the orphanage ministry budget.

When she told Sandeep what Anatoly said, Sandeep rolled his eyes and said his children only received a fraction of what the Goa kids got. The next morning after English class, Nadya, Kavita, and Alexandra traveled by horse-drawn rickshaw to a store in downtown Goa to buy yarn and other material for the children. For the next week or so, the women spent hours knitting wool hats, sweaters, and gloves every day. In addition, we adults put up plastic sheets over every place in the house where cold air could enter, while Sandeep and Paul bought some coal, which we lit in tin cans to try to warm the home as much as possible. We also continued lighting fires during the afternoons. Through it all, the children never complained, although the women had to replace more than one missing glove. The knitting never stopped for about the next two months.

Aside from English classes, the children drew pictures and helped with the laundry. The wet clothes were hung to dry on the second-floor roof, where there was a clothesline and plenty of room to sit in the sunshine. I had no idea how to teach them cricket, probably the most popular sport in India, but I taught them soccer and checkers. We also played lots of Uno games. At the same time, Sandeep had been teaching the children math. All the questions were very elementary, however, and I could see Milan, Moses, and Rashikant were bored. I told Sandeep I could teach them multiplication and how to do addition, subtraction, and division using larger numbers. After that, the three older boys and I had math class every afternoon in the big room. Since math was my worst subject in school, you could say this was a real miracle, although I think the boys enjoyed having private time with their American "uncle."

A few weeks before Christmas, a UPS truck stopped outside the orphanage and dropped off a box. Inside was a stack of Hindu Bible storybooks sent by the Samaritan's Purse organization as part of its Operation Christmas Child. It was one of those gifts a lot of American and other Western kids would have yawned at and put on a shelf to gather dust. However, for the Bareilly children, it was probably the only Christmas present they had ever received. Their eyes sparkled, and their mouths opened into huge smiles as they clutched their new book. Later, you could see them reading their books any chance they got.

Despite the bright points, Nadya and I felt bottled up inside the house. Alexandra didn't have much interest in interacting with people outside, but Nadya and I did. Nadya mentioned the Bible study idea to Sandeep, but he adamantly opposed it. He feared anything he thought would raise the profile of the orphanage and possibly create trouble with Hindu or Muslim neighbors. The orphanage sat in a tiny sliver of land surrounding the Catholic church and school containing most of Bareilly's tiny Christian minority. The area to the north and west of the orphanage was primarily Hindu, while to the east and south was largely Muslim. There had been some violence between Hindus and Muslims in the city a couple of years before, but there seemed to be a sort of truce when we were there. There also appeared to be sort of a tacit agreement between Hindus and Christians that allowed Christians to worship freely as long as they didn't proselytize. A few years earlier, a couple of Christians had been beaten up near the church while passing out evangelistic tracts.

Nadya and I went out anyway. One of the first places we went was about a half-mile to the south of the orphanage, where we walked past an old, dilapidated stone house and an open field where women were squatting on the ground, forming cow and horse manure into patties to be used for heating. Many passersby, meanwhile, stared at us, not out of anger or prejudice, but curiosity. Bareilly isn't high on the list for most international travelers, so it was unusual for locals to see a couple of white Europeans walking down the road. Soon, we reached a market area and found a small store where we bought some fruit and snacks. The owner, Amir, became one of our friends. Up the road a short distance, we met an older man with a hard lifetime chiseled in the wrinkles on his face who was selling peanuts from a horse-drawn wagon. He couldn't speak a word of English, but we developed a friendship, and his peanuts became a favorite snack.

Another time, Nadya and I went to get some art and school supplies for the children from another store in the same market area. The problem was neither of the two employees spoke English, and neither Nadya nor I could speak Hindi. Fortunately, Kamil, the owner of a jewelry shop across the hall, overheard our conversation and came to help. He spoke English at a native level and told the shop workers what we needed.

Kamil also became friends and invited us to his house for dinner one evening. Sandeep and Kavita were worried we would say too much about the orphanage and cause trouble, but nothing like that happened. Instead, as we neared Kamil's house, neighbors swarmed the car to get a close look at us. Westerners rarely visited their neighborhood, and they looked at us like celebrities. Inside the house—which had heat and air conditioning and glass in the windows—Kamil's wife and other family members were dressed in formal attire and stood next to a table draped with an elegant red tablecloth and laden with tons of Indian food. Following dinner, we went to another room where Kamil had set up his computer to allow his father, who lived in another city in India, to talk to us on Skype. The father said it was an honor to have Western visitors and thanked us profusely for coming. He added, "Today is a great day in the history of our family." Soon after that, Kamil drove us back to the orphanage.

One chilly late afternoon around that time, Sandeep came up to the second floor where Nadya, Alexandra, and I were talking.

He was carrying a paper bag filled with a dumpling-looking food we had never tried before. It turned out these pieces of divine deliciousness are called "samosa," a fried or baked pastry filled with spiced potatoes, onions or other vegetables, cheese, and beef or other meats. After finishing only one, Nadya and I wanted to know where he got them so we would know the destination of our next field trip. Sandeep gave us some general directions.

Soon after that, Nadya and I left one afternoon in quest of samosa. We often had nothing else to do in the afternoons as the electric grid couldn't handle the demand and the power went off for hours at a time. In Bareilly, we were generally without electricity from mid-morning to late afternoon or early evening. It also wasn't unusual for the power to go off at night, which meant we needed flashlights and candles to see. Businesses and wealthier people had generators, but poorer people had to survive without them.

Instead of turning left toward the market area like we usually went, we turned right onto a winding street. On one side of the road were the usual small stores, while on the other side stood a brick wall surrounding the large Hindu temple where all the weddings took place about six weeks before. Beside a gate leading to the temple, a few women were standing, selling what looked like colorful floral leis. A couple of bicyclists passed by. A few minutes later, we saw what we were looking for: a store with a large cauldron in front where some men were placing samosa in boiling oil.

One of the men saw us looking at the samosa and invited us inside the store. In his early 20s, he introduced himself as Mohit and said he was getting a master's degree in physical education from an Indian university. His parents owned the shop, a narrow space a little smaller than an average American living room which served as a combination bakery, dairy, restaurant, and convenience store. Between his studies and working at the store, he usually got about four hours of sleep a night.

Mohit, who spoke perfect English, asked us to sit down in a couple of plastic chairs and brought us some bottled water and pastries from the bakery. Nadya and I got the hint he wished us to hang around and talk, so we were in no hurry. Mohit intended to get his physical education degree to find ways to improve the fitness of the Indian people. As one example, he lamented that very few Indians are world-class athletes, and the only world championship India usually wins is in cricket, which he described as not very demanding physically. After that, he asked Nadya and me about our-selves and why we were in Bareilly. When we told him we were teaching English at a small Christian orphanage nearby, he said he had no idea such an orphanage existed but thought it was a great idea. Probably an hour later, however, Nadya and I said we really needed to leave. Mohit filled a bag with samosa for the adults and another bag of treats for the kids (we often bought snacks for the children). When I asked how much, Mohit said, "There is no charge today in hopes that you will return soon." I replied that would be no problem.

In fact, I often visited Mohit after that, sometimes alone. In a short time, we became close enough where we could have serious discussions. I found he was a devout Hindu who regularly attend-ed the temple across the street. As I admitted I knew next to noth-ing about Hinduism, I asked him about some of its basic teachings. I told him that Nadya and I were Christ-followers and asked him what he understood about Christianity. I proceeded to basically share the Gospel narrative with him. It was all very friendly and respectful, but after I finished speaking, I was amazed that I said it all within 20 or 30 yards of a Hindu temple. I still remember and pray for Mohit.

I returned from Mohit's store and saw a car parked in front of the orphanage. When I went inside, all the adults were sitting in a circle talking to an Indian man. Sandeep said the man worked for another ministry that rescued four orphan children, three girls and one boy, off the streets of New Delhi and was looking for a new home for them. The organization thought a more rural city such as Bareilly could be a better place for them than a large metropolis like New Delhi. After some discussion, Sandeep agreed to take them. The man said he would return with the children in a few days.

As promised, the man returned later that week. He parked in the street and made his way toward the house. Trailing behind were the four children dressed in sweatshirts and sweatpants and carrying large gym bags. They all entered the large room, where the children dropped their belongings and sat on the floor. Their dazed eyes glared into the distance but focused on nothing. Sand-eep unzipped the bags and rummaged through the clothes inside. The other man spoke a few words before he returned to his car and drove away. Meanwhile, the regular orphanage children stood at one side of the room during this whole process. As the natural leader, Moses walked up to the new children and smiled. "My name is Moses," he said. They gave no reaction, so Moses backed away.

For most of that first day, the boy and the three girls huddled among themselves and said nothing. We soon learned they were brother and sisters. The oldest child was a girl named Shanti (pronounced "Shahn-TEE"). She was probably 12 or 13, tall for her age, and almost entirely skin and bones. As the oldest, she was the boss and asserted her authority over her younger siblings. The next oldest was a girl about ten years old named Anu (pronounced "Ah-NOO"). The next oldest was a boy, probably about 8. His name was Ravi. The youngest was a girl of about six years old named Mahima (pronounced "MA-hee-ma"). The first reaction we adults had was to pity the poor children. That soon changed.

Before English class the next morning, the children were playing with balloons outside the meeting room. Nadya and I had no trouble getting our regulars to sit down for class, but we had to coax the newcomers. Nadya briefly explained the routine to them and began. In a little while, she had the children write something in their notebooks. We always suspected Shanti couldn't read or write, and she made Anu write for her. A few minutes later, the four new children stood up, walked out of the room, and resumed playing with the balloons. I went after them and was unsuccessfully trying to get them to return to class when Kavita came out of the kitchen where she was preparing the kids' morning snack. In an angry voice, the normally petite, mild-mannered Kavita emphasized the importance of education to the children and ordered them back to the classroom. At the time, I figured the new children might have never been in school before and had no idea how to react to instruction.

The problem didn't go away, however. Over the next few days, Shanti refused to come to class, so Kavita gave her an ultimatum: learn English or help her with the cleaning and laundry. Shanti chose cleaning and laundry.

That was disappointing, but more was to come. Not long after the new children arrived, Moses, Milan, and Rashikant went to Sandeep's room one night to tell him Shanti and Anu had been hitting and picking on Sumit, Suraj, and the other younger children. Sandeep confronted Shanti and Anu, but they denied it. Sandeep told Nadya and me about the visit at lunch the next day, and I asked the boys about it at math class that afternoon. They told me the same story. I automatically believed them because I couldn't imagine any of those three had ever lied in their lives. I began to monitor the children's afternoon playtime, and although there were no fights, I did have to stop Shanti, Anu, and Mahima from stealing things like coloring books and crayons from the other kids.

The last straw for Sandeep came one day when he discovered food missing from the refrigerator. He called all the children together and explained that the orphanage didn't have a lot of money, so every bit of food they bought had to feed everyone. If someone stole something, someone else would have to do without. He asked the seven regulars if they did it, and they denied it. The four new kids also denied it at first until Ravi said Shanti and Anu talked Mahima into taking the food. Punishment for Shanti and Anu was quick and severe, a spanking. Sandeep warned Alexandra, Nadya, and me to lock our rooms when we were away to prevent the possibility of thefts.

Not long after that, Sandeep received two phone calls. The first was from Anatoly, and the second was from Brother Caleb, the director of an Indian Pentecostal organization affiliated with the orphanage ministry. Both said they discovered the children came from the state of Bihar, and, more importantly, their parents were still alive. How the children ended up in New Delhi with the other ministry remained uncertain, although some of the Indian ministry leaders I met told me desperate parents sometimes sold children they couldn't afford. However, Anatoly and Brother Caleb told Sandeep the family now wanted their children back and would call him later.

Meanwhile, Ravi had been showing a lot of potential. He was interested in learning English and was good at art and math. Away from his sisters, he had a wonderful personality. Nadya and I suggested a possible solution was to let each child decide whether he or she wanted to stay.

That night, a woman who said she had documentation proving she was the children's mother and a man who claimed to be her brother called Sandeep. Sandeep asked about the father.

"My sister has made several unfortunate romantic mistakes in her life, and this was one of them," the man said. "He has taken a new wife and now lives elsewhere."

"However," the man continued, "perhaps if we reach some satisfactory agreement, you can continue having custody of the children."

"You mean pay you for them?" Sandeep asked.

"Only a small amount..."

Sandeep said, "No deal," and told him to come to get the children. The man said it would be a while before he and his sister could scrape up enough money to pay the train fare for the roughly 500-mile trip from Bihar to Bareilly.

Sandeep told us about the conversation the next morning. He said the mother and the man knew no English, and they were barely fluent in their native language. They likely released their children to the street to make it on their own and steal for the adults at home. Nadya and I still thought we should give each child the choice of staying.

When the man and woman arrived at the Bareilly train station, Sandeep picked them up and drove them to the orphanage. As they walked through the doorway wearing faded, tattered clothes, Sandeep spoke in English to Nadya and me so the man and woman couldn't understand. Basically, he characterized them as uneducated, unscrupulous bumpkins. Kavita had already told the four children to be in the room before Sandeep returned. The eyes of the three girls shone, while Ravi frowned, stuck his hands in his pockets, and stared at the floor. Strangely, I thought, the mother sat in a chair and made no effort to embrace her children. Mahima, Ravi, Anu, and Shanti stood across the room without making a move toward her. I tried to imagine what was going through their minds but could find no answer. The four youths had only lived a short time, but they had already experienced too many of the world's harsh realities.

Sandeep told the children their mother and the man came to take them home, but any of the children who wanted to stay and take advantage of getting an education could remain. Anu shouted, "If I can go home, I will make a sacrifice to my god ten times a day!" The girls all nodded their heads in agreement. Ravi remained quiet. His lips tensed. Shanti and Anu stared at him as Shanti formed a fist and pressed it against Ravi's nose. "I'll go," he whispered, his eyes still fastened to the floor.

You could almost see the smoke coming from Sandeep's collar. Fire blazed from his eyes. "Let's go," he shouted. He, Kavita, Nadya, and the four children left the room to gather the children's belongings and pack their bags.

While they were away, I sat alone with the mother and the man. A momentary thought crossed my mind to say something profound and super-transcendent to them, but they would have never understood me anyway. Instead, I reasoned, why waste a once-in-a-lifetime opportunity like this to exercise my "spiritual gifts" of sarcasm and satire? I had the sensation Hank Aaron must have felt when a pitcher threw a slow, hanging curveball at him over the center of the plate. There was no way I could let this pitch get past me. Knowing they didn't speak a word of English, I looked at them squarely in the eyes, smiled, and chuckled. "You know," I said with a grin, "you two are the biggest rednecks I've ever seen!" I laughed again. They looked at each other and broke out in laughter. I stopped just long enough to add, "If I had my way, you'd be in jail right now." I started laughing even harder, and they echoed me.

About the time the noise died down, the others returned. Sandeep asked me to accompany him and the family to the train station. After he and I loaded the bags in the tiny Suzuki trunk, I sat in front with him as he drove, and the six family members squeezed together in the back seat. We parked in the lot outside the station. It didn't take Sandeep and me long to get their luggage out of the trunk and place it on the ground. The man stood next to us, cupping his hands as if he were begging for money. "Go!" Sandeep yelled, pointing toward the station. As soon as the adults and children were a few steps away from the car, Sandeep pulled out and sped back to the orphanage. We never heard from them again.

That winter, Sandeep and Kavita received good news, however. Kavita had been trying to get pregnant for a long time but was never able to conceive. Finally, she announced she was expecting. The kids were especially happy. For Kavita, it meant her parents, who also lived in Bareilly, could see their grandchild. For Sandeep, it confirmed his plans to use the orphanage to train future Christian leaders for India and evangelize northern India, the most unreached part of the country.

Later developments took some of the joy away from the news. Not long after the New Year, Anatoly and Maria came from Goa by train to meet with Sandeep and Kavita. The subject of the brief meeting was money. Anatoly said current funding was insufficient to operate two buildings, which led Tamara and the ministry board to consider merging the orphanages into a single location. Whether that would be in Goa or another place remained to be seen. It was certain, however, the house in Bareilly would be sold.

Sandeep and Kavita pointed out they would be uprooted from home and family at what should be the happiest time of their lives, but Anatoly refused to listen. The move, he promised, would come soon. I tried to console Sandeep with the fact businesses often transfer employees with no regard to family situations. Perhaps a Christian organization should be operated differently, I said, but apparently not. A few days later, Anatoly called Sandeep from Goa with two more bits of news: a decision had been made to merge the orphanages, and he was stepping down as orphanage ministry director. Anatoly would return to Bareilly in a few days with the new director to give details.

One morning not long after that, some of the boys and I were playing soccer on the second-floor roof when a car parked in front of the orphanage. I stopped the game to see who it was. Out of the car stepped Anatoly and another man. Nadya and Alexandra were hanging up laundry but stopped to look. "I know him!" Nadya exclaimed. She said he was Denis, a former pastor in Russia who came to India as a missionary about eight years before. He had spoken at her church in Nizhnevartovsk several times and had driven her to tears with stories and photos of his India ministry.

We went downstairs to meet them. After the usual greetings, Anatoly said he and Denis would like to meet with Sandeep and Kavita in private. Taking the hint, Nadya and I left, but we heard all the details later from Sandeep. In short, the two orphanages would be merged and moved to a house in Bangalore, a city of 8.5 million in south India where Denis already directed an orphanage ministry. Furthermore, Paul and Alexandra would be moved to help at the Goa orphanage until the merger was complete and the house was sold. The kicker was Anatoly placed Denis in direct leadership of the new orphanage, and Sandeep would be, in effect, demoted to a caretaker position. I told Sandeep later, "You've been railroaded." According to the plan, Anatoly would return in February to drive Nadya and me to Goa and then on to Bangalore, where Denis and we could finish getting the new house ready for the seven Bareilly children plus the 12 Goa kids. Sandeep and Kavita were to pack everything in the Bareilly house and arrive in Bangalore by train about a week later. The beds and other furniture would be delivered by truck.

The two people probably affected the most by this were Sandeep and Nadya. For Sandeep, his initial reaction to Denis could be described as dislike at first sight. Sandeep more than once told me, "All he cares about is money," rubbing his thumb and two forefingers together. Sandeep often complained that Denis was always on his cell phone and never interacted with the children. To him, Sandeep said, it was all a business. His deep anger and pain were obvious to see.

Nadya, meanwhile, fell into a deep depression. Some days she went without food and stayed in our room all day except to teach. There were a couple of reasons. Alexandra was still lamenting the fact her husband had divorced her ten years ago and later married another woman. Despite that, she still wanted him back. She often wandered the second floor, muttering words to try to summon the gift of tongues. To Nadya, however, she said things that made it appear she thought she was more "spiritual" than her. Nadya was never specific, however, so I didn't know exactly what Alexandra said. Whatever it was must have hurt Nadya deeply for her to react like that. On the morning she and Paul were to leave, Nadya stayed in bed. When Alexandra asked her to come downstairs and see them off, she said nothing. Much more than that, however, a lot of Anatoly's words and actions left her disillusioned. She realized Anatoly and Maxim actually shared the same prosperity gospel beliefs, but Anatoly played the "good cop/bad cop" routine to make himself look good. From the start of our relationship, Nadya always looked up to him. In contrast to Maxim, he seemed sensible and down-to-earth, yet enthusiastic about sharing Jesus with others. Instead of seeking the spotlight, he worked quietly behind the scenes. Yet, In Nadya's eyes, something changed after we arrived in India. His remarks at the New Delhi restaurant about the Indian people, his lack of concern about the children in the cold weather, and his insensitivity to Sandeep and Kavita's situation tarnished his hero's crown. The realization pierced Nadya's soul.

Anatoly and Denis accompanied Alexandra and Paul to Goa by train. The kids were a little sad to see Alexandra go, but they shed a torrent of tears at losing Paul. Paul was like a big brother to them, often playing with them or doing something like chasing monkeys away from the orphanage or showing the children how to climb the tree across the street.

With Alexandra gone, Nadya helped Kavita even more with cleaning and laundry. I spent more time around the house playing with the children and helping the older boys with their math. A few weeks passed, and in late February, Anatoly returned. Early the next morning, he and I loaded our things in the Suzuki for the 1,500-mile drive to Bangalore, about the same distance as Atlanta to Denver. While Anatoly was tying a couple of suitcases to the top of the car with a rope, Sandeep pleaded with him once more to keep the orphanage in Bareilly. Anatoly replied with a short, "Time to go." Minutes later, Anatoly, Nadya, and I were on our way.

# 7

# INDIA INTERLUDE, PART 2

The plan was to drive to Goa first, spend three days there, and then proceed to Bangalore. Our tiny, three-cylinder Suzuki took us on the narrow, winding road out of Bareilly through several small villages until we entered a modern four-lane highway heading west to New Delhi. A couple of hours later, we crossed a bridge over the River Ganges — a river Hindus consider sacred. In Hindu belief, bathing in the river can bring about the forgiveness of transgressions or salvation. Pilgrims stood in the wide river while others lined up at temples and stands to buy bottles of water from the holy river. About two hours later, Anatoly got a call on his cell phone. Speaking in Russian, he drove with one hand while he gestured with the other. His voice grew louder and louder. As it turned out, the call came from Denis, who said the owner of the house in Bangalore was threatening to void the rental agreement after he learned the home was going to be used as an orphanage. Something else for Anatoly to worry about.

We passed through New Delhi and, in the late afternoon, traversed an area of deserts and low mountains. At one point, a man was leading a camel along the side of the road, the first time I had ever seen a camel outside a zoo. Darkness came, and we found a hotel in Mumbai (the city formerly known as Bombay) where we spent the night. The next day we followed the highway over taller mountains and past some modern cities, aging fortresses, and religious shrines. Along the way, we passed areas of jungle inhabited

97

by tribes largely untouched by outsiders. By nightfall, I could tell we were nearing Goa by all the billboards advertising alcohol. The city is a popular vacation destination for Russian tourists as well as a place where some wealthy Russians live to escape the brutal winters in their homeland. As darkness came, we drove alongside the beach where Laura spent her lonely afternoons. At last, we reached the Goa orphanage. The children were already in bed, so Maria, Alexandra, and Peter greeted us.

Without much else to do for the next three days, Nadya and I spent part of the next morning exploring the neighborhood. In one direction, the beach was about a mile away. We decided to save that until later. Instead, we walked in the other direction and passed many small, wooden houses surrounded by palms and evergreen trees. We spoke to a group of children playing and saw some sari-clad women walking down the road, carrying baskets or jars on their heads.

Colorful and ornate Hindy symbols decorated the exterior walls and doors of the orphanage. There were two floors. The top floor contained the bedrooms and kitchen used by Russians and other European guests. The bottom floor was for the children and Indian staff. Maria said Nadya and I were free to eat Indian food with the Indian children and workers, but the second-floor menu was always Russian and conversation either in Russian or English. Frankly, Nadya and I weren't thrilled with the arrangement as it seemed a little like 19th- or early 20th-century colonialism, where there was a strict separation between white Europeans and natives. We preferred to spend as much time as possible with the Indians.

Nadya and I noticed the sharp difference between the Goa organization and Sandeep's orphanage in Bareilly. For one thing, Sandeep was right; the Goa children had many more clothes and toys, including electronics, than the Bareilly children. The house and the front yard were full of bicycles, roller skates, CD players, soccer balls, and assorted other sports and electronic game equipment. In addition, unlike Bareilly, discipline in Goa was rare except when Maria administered it. Maria also assumed the English-teaching duties after Laura left, and she and Anatoly hired a private math tutor. Some of the children liked learning, but most preferred to spend time with Anatoly at the beach. Once, Anatoly returned from running an errand while Maria was starting an English lesson. About a half-dozen of the children ran up to him, begging to go to the beach. Anatoly picked a couple of them up and started wrestling with them. After a couple of minutes, he agreed to take them to the beach.

"But what about English class?" Maria asked.

"There will always be English class," Anatoly answered. "Today is for the beach!" Maria shrugged her shoulders but said nothing.

Our three days in Goa passed without incident, except we learned the lease on the house in Bangalore had been worked out somehow. Anatoly, Nadya, and I left early in the morning and drove 350 miles south and east across more mountains and through more jungle until we reached Bangalore late that evening. (After we left India, the government changed the city's name to Bengaluru. I've kept the original name since that was the city's name when we were there.) At first glance, Bangalore seemed almost the opposite of Bareilly. Although both cities shared traffic jams, Bangalore's highways were modern, a few skyscrapers soared above downtown, and much less trash lined the streets than in Bareilly. We turned off the main highway onto a street that passed some modest homes, businesses, and restaurants. It seemed like we were at the edge of town when we turned left onto a bumpy dirt street into what looked like a subdivision with houses lining four or five other small dirt streets. All the houses looked very middle class or upper income, featuring the usual square or rectangular design with a flat roof and a gated brick or stone fence. At the end of one of the streets stood the new orphanage.

Nadya and I thought the location was ideal. The house was far away from the crowded city center but only a short walk from a busy street with fruit and vegetable markets, restaurants, and a variety of other stores. Down our street in one direction was a vacant dirt lot shaded on one side by palm trees where the children could play. Three houses sat next to the orphanage, while a vacant lot and two more houses were across the street. Down the street in the other direction were a couple of vacant lots overgrown with weeds and brush and, farther on, a footpath passing through a line of trees and bushes. Beyond the trees was a tent village, where at night you could see campfires and hear talking and singing. The orphanage itself had a small front and back yard with a wide driveway covered by a metal canopy. In the driveway was a covering for a tank that trucks came to fill with water as needed. Water is scarce and expensive in some parts of the world.

Inside, Denis and his wife, Natasha, greeted us. We met them in a large open room with white marble walls and a white marble floor. A big-screen television hung on one wall, and a pair of speakers sat on the floor. In the daytime, light streamed in through a large picture window facing the street. Next to this room was another room used as a dining room, which was lined by an office, a bedroom, a kitchen, and a combination bathroom/laundry room. Dominating the first floor, however, was a large spiral staircase with a wooden railing and marble steps leading to the upper floors. On the second floor was our bedroom, which featured our own private bathroom, and the bedrooms for the children. The third floor contained a small bedroom and office and a doorway leading to the roof, where, as usual, there was a clothesline and plenty of room to sit and catch any breeze that was blowing. We didn't know until then that Denis and his family had been living in this house. It seemed ironic Anatoly lectured Nadya about "suffering for the Lord" when Denis and Natasha lived in such comparative luxury.

Denis, Natasha, and their teenage son and daughter were just finishing moving to a larger home which he said was more "suitable" for their family. The rental mix-up over the new orphanage occurred when Denis persuaded the real estate agent to rent the house to some people he knew who were moving from out of town. However, it somehow slipped his mind to tell the realtor exactly how many people would be living there.

Nadya and I didn't have much to do until Anatoly, Maria, the Goa children, and the furniture arrived a few days later. The children did a lot of the work setting up bunk beds and storing clothes and toys. Later that week, Denis drove Nadya and me in his van to the Victorian-era Bangalore train station in the city center to pick up Sandeep, Kavita, and the Bareilly children. Another Russian couple who Nadya and I had just met traveled in another van. The plan was whoever couldn't fit in Denis's van could go in the other. We drove through a modern downtown area with expensive shops and American fast-food restaurants, then traversed a neighborhood of stately older red-brick homes which looked like they could have been around when a young British Army officer named Winston Churchill was stationed in Bangalore for a few months in 1896. Past that was the train station.

The train arrived on time. All the Bareilly people seemed fine, including Kavita, who had to endure a nearly two-day rail journey while pregnant. Everyone piled into the vans. On the way to the orphanage, a couple of the children got sick and started vomiting. All we could do was tell them to stick their heads out the window and throw up on the street. Nadya and I figured the youngsters came down with motion sickness after being cooped up in the train from Bareilly for more than 40 hours. Finally, we arrived at the orphanage and waited for the truck hauling the belongings from the Bareilly orphanage. It pulled up to the house later that day, and the new Bangalore orphanage was officially opened.

Nadya and I were surprised that the Bareilly and Goa children got along so well. There was a slight problem, however, because Sumit lost his status as the youngest child to a 3-year-old girl from the Goa orphanage who was cute but seemed used to getting her way in everything. Moses even relinquished his position as oldest to an extremely intelligent 12-year-old girl from the Goa orphanage whose name I forgot but who had the nickname "Tiny." English lessons also went well even with the larger class size. Before teaching English, Nadya taught kindergarten and was an expert at handling children. As a result, she gained the Goa children's respect, and discipline was no problem. In addition, Anatoly and Maria arranged for the children to have a math tutor and a teacher in Kannada, the predominant language spoken in the Bangalore region.

Although the children were having success in learning, all the adults agreed they needed to start regular school the next academic term. They couldn't attend while we were there because the orphanages were formed too late for them to enter school that year. The main hurdle was paperwork. Schools would not allow the children to enroll without proper documentation, and some of the children had no papers.

Brother Caleb traveled to Bangalore from New Delhi to talk with Denis and Sandeep about the problem. He summed up his solution in one sentence: "You can get any document you want in India if you have the money." He did what needed to be done, and soon Denis received file folders containing authentic-looking but false birth, medical, and school records for each child. Whoever performed the job was professional enough to slightly yellow some of the pages and crumple the edges of some of the folders to make them appear aged and used. With some haggling, Denis managed to enroll the children in a private Christian school. Although I had misgivings about using fake documents, the children would be getting an education. Without the papers, they would have spent another year out of school. I never heard of any viable alternatives.

Unfortunately, other aspects of life at the orphanage weren't as positive as the children's education and social success. After Anatoly returned to Goa and was unable to serve as a buffer, tensions grew between Sandeep and Denis. Denis took over complete control of our orphanage and another Bangalore orphanage where he served as "pastor." The only duties he left Sandeep were to buy food for the children and conduct nightly devotions.

"It seems like you've been demoted," I told Sandeep when he got the news. I patted him on the shoulder, but you could see the anger and hurt in his eyes. More than that, Denis rarely visited the orphanage except to give his Sunday morning sermon, and I can't remember if he ever spent time with the kids.

The first Sunday afternoon after the children were in Bangalore, we drove to Denis's other orphanage, a house a few miles away. Fairly large, it was surrounded by a tall concrete fence and an arch over the entrance. As we drove up, a swarm of kids played soccer or other games or just hung around. After the customary greetings and a quick tour from the Indian couple who actually ran the orphanage, there was singing, and Denis gave the message, a half-hour dissertation on wealth and giving. The children—many from Myanmar, in addition to India—were less than excited and either yawned or did all they could do to fight off sleep. He asked me to give a short presentation on giving the next week. I knew exactly what he wanted me to say, but, instead, I spoke about ways to give apart from money, such as time, service, and listening. Denis didn't seem to like that. In fact, for the remainder of the time Nadya and I spent in India, every message he gave centered on money.

Later, Sandeep showed Nadya and me a receipt for $300 in purchases Denis and Natasha had made using ministry funds from an expensive grocery store frequented by foreigners and wealthy Indians. Among the items they bought were seafood, gourmet cheeses, and imported shampoo. Nadya made a copy of the receipt and sent it and a description of some more of Denis's activities to Tamara, the woman in Nizhnevartovsk funding and overseeing the orphanage ministry. Despite frequent calls, texts, and emails, however, Nadya never heard from her until much later. I assumed she wouldn't like knowing some of her money was going for gourmet foods for Denis and his family and not to the orphans.

Shortly after our orphanage opened, a middle-aged Russian woman dressed in Indian attire came to the house saying she wanted to see the children. Nadya and I and Sandeep and Kavita thought she looked harmless, so we let her in. Her name was Ludmila, and she had volunteered for Denis at the other orphanage for a number of years. Her English was almost non-existent, so she spoke in Russian to Nadya. She had heard about the new orphanage and wanted to meet the kids. Nadya and Ludmila quickly became friends, and we made plans to have dinner at a nearby restaurant. The main topic was to find out what made Denis tick.

Ludmila came with her teenage son. She said Denis served as a pastor in another Siberian city and was friends with Maxim from the Nizhnevartovsk church. About eight years before, they had some kind of falling out, and, over Natasha's objections, Denis and his family moved to India to serve as missionaries. Moved by Denis's example, Ludmila and her son followed and lived in a small apartment Denis provided. At first, he was a sincere missionary, but donations and ministry results were few. Finances became a problem. He branched out into real estate and tried several get-rich-quick schemes. His tastes grew, so he then had to have the best of everything, food, photography equipment, houses.

Ludmila and her son then made some accusations against him. For example, they described when a particular Russian mission team came to Bangalore to help Denis's ministry for a week. After the first day, Denis and Natasha went on a week-long getaway at a resort in the neighboring Indian state of Kerala. Before leaving, Natasha told the team members they could help her and her husband the most by taking care of the house and watching their children while she and Denis were gone. Other allegations bordered on the illegal, such as a plan supposedly hatched by Anatoly and Denis before Nadya and I were married to try to get her a student visa even though she wasn't applying to an Indian university. This made sense because when I was still in the U.S., Anatoly had told Nadya he was trying to get her a student visa to India. A string of other allegations against Denis followed. Ludmila said she had witnessed everything. From what we had observed of Denis so far, we tended to believe her.

While I was in India, my Russian visa expired. Without it, I couldn't return to Russia. As my wife, Nadya could sponsor my visa application, which was necessary for it to be approved. However, we had to travel 350 miles east by train to apply at the Russian consulate in the Indian city of Chennai. Chennai, formerly known as Madras, is a city of 7 million on the Bay of Bengal and a business, art, and cultural center. After applying, we had to wait a week before my visa would be ready. In the meantime, we took in some of the sights despite the oppressively hot and humid weather. Parts of the city we saw were beautiful, and we toured a Catholic church where supposedly the bones of the Apostle Thomas, who legend says was martyred in India, are buried. However, we also saw lots of trash, homeless people sleeping on the sidewalk, and men urinating on any wall they could find. Garbage lying on the sand and trash, not to mention a drowned dog, floating in the water took away any desire to swim in the ocean.

A week later, with my new Russian visa safely affixed inside my passport, we returned by train to Bangalore. Soon, we learned three women from Maxim's church were coming on a four-day visit to the Bangalore orphanages. Nadya knew them, all wives of financially well-off and, therefore, influential men in the church inner circle. Denis, however, grew paranoid. He became obsessed that Maxim was sending the women to check up on him or even steal his ministry. He accused Nadya of being a spy since she had attended Maxim's church, and he believed she was transmitting false information about him to unidentified others back in Nizhnevartovsk. Denis said all this with me around. I just smiled. For one thing, I could understand more Russian than I let on because it came in handy when teenage students were plotting things in class behind my back. For another, I was married to the best interpreter around. Like many Russians I met, Denis tended to underestimate Americans, so I was glad to play the part of the stereotypical ignorant, naïve American while recording everything for Nadya to use in future reports to Tamara.

The women arrived at the Bangalore airport on a Thursday morning. Denis picked them up and took them to his home, where they stayed in a guest room. Whenever I saw him around them, he acted as the consummate charming host. Two of the women were rather short and probably around 60. The other woman was a tall redhead, probably in her early 40s. Later that day, the women came to the orphanage to lead the children in arts and crafts. Friday, the plan was for the women and children, along with Nadya, Ludmila, and me, to take a bus downtown to tour the science museum — officially the Visvesvaraya Industrial and Technological Museum

—followed by a stop at a nearby park and playground. Saturday was reserved for what the women called a "sports competition" for the kids in the vacant lot down the street, while Sunday evening, a get-together at the other orphanage was planned.

Our Friday began just before mid-morning when Denis dropped the women off at our orphanage. The two older women were dressed reasonably for an outing on a hot day in south India, but the younger woman, wearing a frilly pink dress, white heels, and a big, floppy hat, looked more prepared to sip mint juleps at a Kentucky Derby party than stand beside a dusty road for half an hour waiting on a bus. The children enjoyed the day, however, which was the important thing. Saturday was also successful, as the games went over well.

Sunday, however, was a long day.

In the morning, Denis gave his usual 30-minute money message at our orphanage. The three guests were in attendance, and since Denis spoke in English and the women spoke only Russian, Nadya and I sat in front of them so Nadya could interpret. It was extremely hard for her to repeat a lot of what he said, not linguistically but doctrinally. After speaking, Denis passed around a pouch to put in money for an offering. The pouch soon came around to the children. Bewilderment covered their faces. They looked around the room at the adults to try to determine what they were supposed to do. The children had no idea what the pouch was for, but even more, very few of them had probably ever held a coin in their young lives. Sandeep got up from where he was sitting and whispered something to Moses. After that, the children passed the pouch to each other. With the offering over, Denis gave a quick prayer and finished the service. In the moment of silence that followed, the three women leaped from their chairs and applauded, shouting, "Bravo, pastor! Bravo!" I had been in Russian churches where pastors were applauded after their sermons, but it came as a shock to the Indians there. Across the room, Sandeep's and Kavita's eyes bulged, and their mouths gaped open. They had never witnessed anything like it. I was sickened that a ministry touting to help "the poorest of the poor" would try to get money from children who had never known anything but poverty.

Late in the afternoon, we loaded up and went to the other orphanage. A party was planned for children whose birthdays were that month and to honor the three women on their last night in

Bangalore before returning to Russia. The festivities took place in a huge tent on the orphanage grounds.

First came mountains of food and praise and worship music, complete with colored lights and expensive sound equipment, followed by another financial talk by Denis. He was in rare form, as, among other things, I learned Jesus was actually rich and wore only the nicest clothes. It takes a lot to make me angry, and this was one of those times. I hated the fact that Denis's half-truths, false statements, and verses taken out of context could influence children who didn't know any better.

It got even worse. After the message, chairs and tables were moved away for dancing. At first, there was simple Christian praise music suitable for the children to jump and hop around to, but as the evening progressed, the Christian music was replaced by secular music with suggestive lyrics. The children stood around, bored, and Sandeep and Kavita were planted in place, unsure of what to do. Meanwhile, Denis grinned as he danced with the younger woman while Natasha looked on in silent displeasure.

Finally, Nadya and I had enough. We asked Sandeep and Kavita how they were doing. Of course, they answered with a polite, "Fine." We next told them it was getting late, and the children probably should get to bed. We added that we thought the songs were inappropriate for the kids.

"Are the words about sexual things?" Sandeep asked. I nodded my head yes. "Let's go," he said in the same angry tone of voice he used a couple of months earlier when the man and woman from Bihar left with Shanti, Anu, Ravi, and Mahima.

After the kids were in the car, I asked Sandeep if I could speak at devotions the next evening because I wanted to correct what Denis said. "Please do," Sandeep answered.

With steam still coming out of my ears and from under my collar, I spent half an hour dissecting what Denis said and trying to give the correct interpretation based on Scripture taken in context. I can't remember many of the details now, but I do recall him saying, for example, "Jesus was wealthy. He didn't get his clothes off the rack." I realized some of the children were too young to understand what I was talking about, but I didn't want to take the chance of any bad seed sprouting in their young minds.

Nadya and I were walking along a street near our orphanage one afternoon when we met a woman in her yard. She was Indian, but her English was impeccable. We introduced ourselves, and she invited us to come inside her house. Her name was Mary Grace. Her father was an Indian Army officer during one of India's wars with neighboring Pakistan, and she attended university for a few years in Great Britain. Her husband, Daka, was a member of one of the many indigenous tribes in India.

Daka became a pastor and opened a church in their home. In addition to the usual Sunday morning service, he also conducted Bible studies and outreaches to immigrants and others who migrated to Bangalore from other parts of India. Nadya and I visited the church the next Sunday and were impressed. The people we met seemed warm and genuine, and instead of taking Bible verses out of context to justify greed and materialism, Daka spoke with knowledge and compassion. After that, we permanently ditched Denis's show. We told Sandeep and Kavita about the church, and soon, they and the children started coming. The Sunday health-and-wealth services at the orphanage were over.

The Russian women weren't the only guests the orphanage had, however. Mission groups often stopped by, spent about an hour touring the house, took photos with the children, and left. That evening, their social media pages would be filled with heartfelt stories and pictures of helping the "poor orphan children." An example happened once when Anatoly pulled up in a minibus with ten seminary students from Moscow. The students were planning to spend a week in India and wanted to see the children as part of their mission experience. The seminarians walked in, took some photos with the kids, and left. No more than 15 minutes elapsed from when the students got off the minibus until they got back on. Anatoly said they would spend the rest of the week in Goa. After they left, I told Nadya they should be called "missionary tourists."

Unfortunately, troubles continued after the debacle with the Russian women, especially the rift between Indians and Russians in this particular orphanage ministry. One day when Brother Caleb was visiting the orphanage to talk to Sandeep, he asked to meet with Nadya and me. He told us he was tired of all the Russians and Ukrainians in leadership in orphanage ministry. He made an exception for Nadya because he had heard only good things about her from Sandeep and Kavita.

In a few minutes, he changed subjects. "There is a lot of work to do here in South India," he said, "but Northern India is our country's great mission field." He concluded by asking me if I would consider being a missionary in Northern India? I thanked him but answered I really couldn't at that time in my life. I believed Nadya and I had more to do in Russia.

Nadya grew more and more disillusioned with the India ministry, and I came to the point where I had seen enough. Therefore, we made flight reservations to return to Russia in mid-April, only a few weeks away. While we were making our plans, I realized this would be another step in faith. Our apartment owner's son would be released soon, and we would have to find a new apartment. We would also need to find new students to help us make it financially through the summer.

Nadya smiled at me and patted my cheek before replying, "God takes care of crazy people like us."

Our final days in India were happy but tinged in sadness at the prospect of leaving Sandeep, Kavita, and the children. English class became more games and singing than structured lessons, and there was lots of playtime in the warm South India sun. The children drew artwork and wrote goodbye cards for us before the last photos were taken.

Finally, the day came to go to the airport. Except for our heavy suitcase, which I got to lug, the kids fought over who carried our other bags down the stairs to load in the car. Sandeep drove us to the Bangalore airport. It wasn't a long drive, but long enough to catch one more peek at the countryside and small Indian villages along the way and get in some last-minute chatting. When we arrived at the terminal, Sandeep parked beside the curb, and we unloaded our bags. Before Nadya and I walked away, Sandeep said he had one more thing he wanted to tell us: "We've had lots of volunteers from all over the world, but you were the only ones who really loved the children."

Words seemed superfluous after that. Nadya and I boarded a domestic flight from Bangalore to New Delhi, then took a shuttle bus to the international terminal for a non-stop, six-and-a-half-hour flight on Aeroflot, the Russian national airline, from New Delhi to Moscow. From Moscow, we would take a train to St. Petersburg.

In the sky between India and Russia, Nadya and I reviewed the five months we spent in Bareilly and Bangalore. We recalled some of our most vivid memories. The roads clogged with cars, trucks, buses, motorcycles, all honking their horns at once. The aroma of Indian spices coming from restaurants. The constant sounds of Hindi music coming loudspeakers. Lines of cattle and goats walking along the street. The chatter of buyers and sellers in outdoor produce markets. The sight of homeless people curled up and sleeping on the sidewalks. The early-morning calls to prayer from mosques and the all-night wedding parties at Hindu temples. Encountering belief systems we had never dealt with before. The still-unanswered questions about the raggedly dressed children we saw playing in the busy street our first day in New Delhi.

Most of all, we remembered the orphanage children. Sumit's missing two front teeth. Suraj's mischievous smile. Milan's artistic sensitivity. Moses's prodigal wisdom. We also thought of the leaders. Kavita's quiet hospitality combined with her strength to be firm when necessary. Sandeep's passion for reaching Northern India with the Gospel mixed with his deep pride. Brother Caleb's difficult choice that enabled the children to enroll in school.

Nadya and I thought that our impact on the children and the relationships we developed outside the orphanages were positive. Although we witnessed a ministry doing a lot of things the wrong way, we realized there were many other ministries in India, such as the church Daka and Mary Grace organized in Bangalore, sincerely helping people in love and truth. We also experienced a bit of the diverse cultural blend that constitutes India. We saw the range of extreme wealth to extreme poverty. We observed friendliness juxtaposed against social ills that were often overlooked. We felt privileged to be able to spend five months in what we came to consider the most unique country in the world.

Much later, the thought crossed my mind that a lot of what Nadya and I did in India could be done by anyone, anywhere. Develop friendships with people you see every day, especially those society tends to forget. Volunteer time to tutor a child in reading, math, or any other school subject in which they need help. Go out of your way to meet someone from a different race, religion, or nationality. Pray for the people God brings in your path. Practice seeing the world through the eyes of Jesus.

Our plane landed in Moscow on an overcast Sunday morning. A few patches of snow remained on the grass next to the runway. The pilot taxied the plane toward the terminal, but he stopped not more than 50 yards from the gate. Everyone remained seated, but we all wondered what was the problem. Passengers craned their necks to peek through the windows, but nothing was happening outside.

A few more minutes passed before a flight attendant got on the intercom and announced with a bit of contempt in Russian-accented English, "Ladies and gentlemen, our delay is caused by the incompetence of the ground crew."

Under my breath, I snickered softly. Gone were the polite, respectful conversations we enjoyed at the orphanage. We were back in Russia.

# 8

# BACK TO RUSSIA

After clearing customs at the airport, Nadya and I took a taxi to the train station where we would be leaving for St. Petersburg that night. We had a few hours to kill, so we left our luggage in a big locker we rented at the station and went for a quick tour of Moscow. The main place I wanted to see was Red Square, the historic square in the center of Moscow that contains such iconic landmarks as Lenin's Tomb, St. Basil's Cathedral, and the east wall of the Kremlin.

It was too far to walk to Red Square, but there was a metro entrance on the other side of a busy street. As we were waiting for the crossing light to change, dozens of cars and trucks passed by. Yet, something seemed strange to my ears. "Do you hear that?" I asked Nadya.

"What?"

I smiled. "Silence."

For the first time in five months, we were able to stand on a street corner without hearing constant honking from car or truck horns or shouts from street vendors pleading for customers. Strangely, a busy street in the capital of Russia, a city of around 12 million, was quieter on a late Sunday morning than some of the places we visited in India. That's not to say either was better, simply different. Before we left for India, I was still going through the stages of culture shock I experienced after arriving in Russia: honeymoon, frustration, acceptance, and adaptation. However, life in India was so different from the West that I began to think the cultural gap between the U.S. and Russia wasn't that big. Although I was becoming more accustomed to Russian life, I was still out of my comfort zone and facing new challenges. Plenty more were on their way.

Spring was in the air when Nadya and I arrived in St. Petersburg the next day. The sun peeked out from behind the clouds more often, tiny buds appeared on tree limbs, and little sprigs of green grass started emerging from the ground. We had missed the St. Petersburg winter.

Not long after we got home, Nadya finally heard from Tamara, the orphanage foundation director in Nizhnevartovsk, after many unsuccessful attempts to reach her when we were in India. She told Nadya she had received her messages and documentation. After reviewing the information, she removed Denis as well as Sandeep and Kavita from their positions, and placed the children in another Christian orphanage in Northern India. Denis landed on his feet and continued his ministry with the other Bangalore orphanage. Sandeep and Kavita returned to Bareilly, where a few months later, Kavita gave birth to a baby girl. Anatoly lingered in India a while longer before he returned to Russia. Soon after that, he sent out a mass email seeking donors for a new aid organization he had established to help people in need. We didn't have much contact with any of these people after our return to Russia.

However, a couple of friends who were inspired by our trip to India went themselves within the next couple of years and visited the children. The kids all said they remembered us and missed us.

Everything at the apartment remained the same as when we left, although a short time after we returned, Nadya received word from the apartment owner that her son was being released from prison and we would have to move. Nadya found a reasonably priced, modern apartment in a complex not far from where we were living. The location was close to a grocery store and shopping center, about a 15-minute walk to the nearest metro station, and an even closer walk to a tram stop. Along with comfortable furniture, the apartment even had a television with cable included in the rent.

The other major event that spring was Nadya's daughter, Rita, getting married. She and her groom, Timofey ("Timothy" in English), had their ceremony in a different wedding palace than the one where Nadya and I were married, but the building, just down the street from the American and German consulates, was still as opulent as the one where Nadya and I were married. Following the ceremony was a dinner for the families at a nearby restaurant. I gained a Russian daughter and son-in-law to go with my American son and daughter, Tim and Esther.

My teaching routine remained about the same as before the five months in India. I got up early in the morning, crossed the tram tracks, an open field, and two busy streets to reach the metro station. Next to the station were various kinds of small restaurants, bakeries, markets, and other stores. To practice my Russian, I occasionally bought lunch or snacks from the bakery and a couple of the restaurants. The station itself, named Avtovo (pronounced "AHV-ta-va"), was ranked as one of the 12 most beautiful subway stations in the world. Overall, the theme for the station is the defense of Leningrad during the Nazi siege of the city in World War II. Outside, there is a cupola on top with a row of classical Greek or Roman columns in front. Inside, passengers walk down steps to the platform, where chandeliers hang from the ceiling and rows of ornate glass columns stand. A mural of a woman holding a child symbolizing peace is at the end of the platform, while the platform walls are lined with metallic hammers and sickles, left from when the building was finished in 1955.

Most days, I boarded the metro before the morning rush to teach classes at businesses in different parts of St. Petersburg. One of my favorite classes was with employees at the Russian branch of a Silicon Valley internet technology corporation who were taking English lessons to communicate better with their California colleagues. I hope I helped them improve their English as much as I learned from them about possible future applications of technology. I also got a little insight into the Russian philosophy of technology. "Russians may not invent much software," one employee told me, "but we have the best hackers." Another fun group consisted of high school students I taught at a language school where I led many classes and conversation groups. In addition, I taught quite a few students at the apartment.

The story of another prized pupil began that summer when I received an email from a language school where I often worked asking if I would be interested in teaching a 6-year-old girl who lived close to Nadya and me. The girl's mother was an IT engineer in Silicon Valley, while her daughter, Elena, lived with her grandparents. The mother contacted the school because she wanted Elena to take English lessons from an American teacher before joining her in California.

I had never taught English to someone so young, but I had no problem getting paid for taking on a new challenge. However, the school had no idea what level of English Elena spoke, so the people there gave me all kinds of beginning English worksheets, puzzles, and other items for children. Nadya also provided me with plenty of children's materials. When I arrived at the grandparents' apartment building and pressed the buzzer at the entrance, I was a little nervous, but the grandmother greeted me warmly, and I began. As it turned out, Elena had visited California before and already knew lots of English. In fact, I reported to the school that she knew more English than many of my adult students. In addition, since her grandfather was a physics professor at a university in the Soviet days and her mother had worked as an engineer, I figured she had some intelligent DNA.

Still, Elena had the attention span of a typical 6-year-old, making it a challenge to find enough activities to engage her active — sometimes overactive — mind. We spent most of the time playing games, watching videos, and singing songs, all in English. For a month, I taught Elena for one hour, five afternoons a week. I soon became almost part of the family. The grandmother wouldn't let me leave when each lesson was over without having tea and snacks, and despite my elementary Russian and the grandparents' broken English, we had nice conversations and became friends. After the last lesson, Elena's grandparents gave me a calendar with attractive photos of St. Petersburg along with a few other gifts. It marked the first time anyone had ever given me a gift as a teacher.

My favorite part of teaching English after Nadya and I returned from India, however, was a special conversation group I formed. Although the conversation groups organized by language schools were helpful, they could be less than exciting, mainly because schools usually chose threadbare topics for discussion such as favorite books or movies, tips for learning languages, or understanding new cultures. After a while, both students and leaders grew tired of them.

Over time, however, I met students who shared my love of history, and I had the thought of starting my own history discussion group in English. Unlike the school-sponsored groups, this one would be for free. Almost everyone I mentioned the idea to said they loved it. Up to 10 or 12 crammed into our living room at times, but there was a core group of five or six regulars. First, there was Michael, the IT employee I helped prepare for a job interview in English. He had served in the Russian army missile corps and was primarily interested in military history. There was also Nastya, Michael's teenage daughter, who I think mainly came to rein in her father when discussions got a little too exciting; Katerina, who worked in a travel office and had been one of my students; and Natalie, a lawyer. Sometimes Natalie's husband, a graduate student in automotive technology and an expert on all things concerning tanks and submarines, had time to come. One man who visited a few times had moved to St. Petersburg from the Caspian Sea region and belonged to the Kalmyk people group, the only Buddhist people group in Europe. He could tell you the exact time and date in 1943 when Stalin's troops came and herded the Kalmyks onto train cars to transport them to Siberian labor camps.

The original plan was to meet for an hour and a half every other Saturday afternoon. However, everyone had such a great time we decided to get together every Saturday. Pretty soon, our meetings also expanded to two or three hours.

We discussed topics ranging from the Cold War to the 1917 Russian Revolution to ancient history. The group, however, seemed most interested in U.S. history, and I was glad to try to clear up a few of the misconceptions about American history and culture. For example, because everyone in the group was either Russian Orthodox or professed atheist, I included the influence of the Protestant Reformation on Western thinking prior to the American Revolution (which provided me with a handy way to explain the Gospel), and we had an interesting discussion comparing serfdom in tsarist Russia with slavery in the Americas.

I never knew one misconception existed until I was in Russia. I discovered many Russians are still bitter over the Alaska Purchase, which barely gets a mention in most U.S. history books, and a number of false ideas in Russian popular media have sprung up around it. One said the purchase was actually a 99-year lease, and another said the ship carrying the gold from the U.S. to pay for Alaska sank in the Gulf of Finland on the way. I found a copy of the original agreement and the check for $7.2 million from the U.S. Treasury, but when I showed them to some Russians I knew, they refused to believe they were authentic. Most of all, many Russians blame Empress Catherine II, better known as Catherine the Great, for the sale. Katerina said her parents intentionally gave her the name "Katerina" instead of the Russian "Ekaterina" because they didn't want to name their daughter after the person who "gave Alaska to the Americans." However, I showed her and the rest of the group that it was Tsar Alexander II, about a century after Catherine the Great, who sold Alaska to the U.S. in 1867. The information shocked Katerina, and she said she would have to tell her parents they named her "Katerina" for nothing.

People in the group were also fascinated with American Indians and asked about Indian reservations and other aspects of Native American life. When I showed them videos of Plains tribes and the Cherokees in the Great Smoky Mountains, they commented how similar their language, dress, and customs were to Siberian groups. Some of the interchanges between Natalie, with her logical legal mind, and Michael, with his love for historical theories lying outside the mainstream, such as lost civilizations and extraterrestrial contact, provided comic relief.

Of all my groups in St. Petersburg, this was my favorite. I not only developed deep friendships, but I also probably learned more from the others than they learned from me. Even though the effects of culture shock had subsided, I was still encountering plenty of frustrations about my new home, but our discussions and their answers to many of my questions helped me adapt easier.

About a month after our return from India began what St. Petersburg calls its "White Nights." Because the city lies so far north, from mid-May to mid-July, the sun stays above the horizon for almost 24 hours a day. Close to the summer solstice, there is hardly any darkness at all. If I taught a night class during White Nights, the sun would still be out even if I got home at 10 or 11 p.m. Especially on Saturday nights, Nadya and I sometimes took a late-night stroll down Nevsky Prospekt, the main thoroughfare through the tourist district, or along one of the canals. In India, we had spent almost every moment together, but back in Russia, we usually only had late nights and Sundays alone. I was usually booked up Monday through Saturday with classes for intermediate to advanced students. Nadya taught children's classes at one particular private language school and usually didn't get home until 9 or 10 p.m. She also taught many elementary-level adult students. If she came home at night after me, I tried to have dinner waiting for her. Nadya called me her "golden retriever" because, like the dog breed, I really wanted to please her. Nothing made me feel worse than disappointing her.

One problem I had was I always felt tired. I'm a day person, so it's hard for me to sleep when the sun is out. More than that, however, I couldn't relax. Maybe it was all the new sensations and information I was taking in, or maybe it was because I was still adjusting to my new environment. Other new English teachers I met also shared the same feeling I had of being watched all the time. In time, that sensation went away, but it was real in my first couple of years in Russia.

To me, a couple of events each summer symbolized the extremes I noticed in St. Petersburg. The first was the Scarlet Sails in late June, a spectacular show which began in 1968 to celebrate the end of the school year. The festival features a pirate battle, red-sailed boats floating down the Neva River, numerous concerts, and fireworks. Entertainment includes performances by the St. Petersburg Philharmonic Orchestra and the Mariinsky Ballet and such popular performers as the Cirque du Soleil and Antonio Banderas. As many as 3 million people line the river to watch the event.

On one end of the spectrum was Airborne Forces Day, commonly known as Paratroopers' Day. Observed throughout Russia on August 2nd each year, all past and present Russian military paratroopers celebrate... well, I'm not sure what. However, packs of paratroopers fill the streets and metro, waving flags, singing, drinking, swimming in fountains, and picking fights. Mostly drinking. The first or second summer I was in Russia, a newspaper article reported a man living in one Siberian town was arrested on Paratroopers' Day after police accused him of dishonoring veterans by not being drunk enough. On my first Paratroopers' Day in St. Petersburg, I happened to be riding the metro when a fight broke out between two inebriated paratroopers who managed to land a few punches even though they could barely stand. Some Russian friends advised me that it's a good day for foreigners to lay low and stay close to home.

When I was in St. Petersburg, autumn could be rainy, but the sunny days between showers were worth the wait. The colors in the leaves matched the crispness in the air, and the city returned to work and school after the White Nights.

Eventually, winter comes, and Russians celebrate their major holiday, New Year's. In Russia and other Orthodox countries,

Christmas Day falls on January 7th and is strictly a religious holiday, although many people, including English teachers, still work that day. (Russians call December 25th "Catholic Christmas.") The big celebration is New Year's Eve, a combination of Independence Day, Thanksgiving, and Christmas rolled into one. In the weeks leading up to the day, streets and homes are decorated, parties are thrown, and stores are packed with shoppers. The trees and lights on Nevsky Prospekt are amazing, especially if it's snowing at night. Children await the arrival of *Ded Moroz* (Grandfather Frost) and his granddaughter, *Snegurochka* (the Snow Maiden), to deliver their gifts.

The New Year's after we arrived from India was the first we spent at Rita's in-laws' dacha north of St. Petersburg. The customs there were probably similar to other Russian families. Around 10 p.m., everyone gathered to eat a massive meal with many traditional Russian dishes consisting of various types of fish, salads, breads, baked goods, and lots else. After eating is the time to open gifts. Everything stopped at midnight to watch Vladimir Putin give his annual three-minute New Year's address to the nation on TV, followed by a recording of a choir singing every — and I mean every — verse of the Russian national anthem. After that, kids, parents, and grandparents played some more while the night was capped off with fireworks, no matter how cold it was outside. New Year's Day was rather tame in comparison, and Russian TV always shows a lot of old Soviet-era comedy films. Some are pretty good. Rita's in-laws always treated me with lots of kindness and hospitality.

Besides cold, ice, and snow, the other negative to St. Petersburg winter is darkness. From November to April, the weather is generally overcast, gloomy, wet, and usually snowy. Around the winter solstice, sunrise is between 9:30 and 10 a.m., with sunset between 3:30 and 4 p.m. Places even farther north on Russia had almost no sunlight in the winter. The constant winter darkness seemed to affect Nadya so much I mentioned to her that she might have Seasonal Affective Disorder. I told her that someone I worked with once was diagnosed with SAD and went in for regular light treatments during the winter.

More than the darkness, Nadya was also getting tired of the cold. She came up with a possible solution, however. First, she researched and found there was a need for English teachers in South Russia near where she was born and where temperatures would be much warmer. Second, she thought it would be feasible to start our own language school there. At the time, the plan seemed reasonable to me. I made a mistake here because I went along without asking some hard questions just so I would please Nadya. For example, I didn't ask about living expenses, property availability, and whether there was actually demand for another language school. This was one area where our normally excellent communication broke down.

Over the winter and spring, we prepared for another location change. Of course, Nadya's mother and sister, who lived in the area, thought moving nearby was a great idea. The main thing we needed to decide was where we would live and establish the school. We figured the two most likely places to start a school in that area would be either Novorossiysk, a city on the Black Sea coast, or Krasnodar, the largest city in the region. We finally planned to stay with Nadya's sister in the city of Krymsk — where Nadya and I arrived by train on our wedding trip — and use that as a base to tour both cities and choose which one we thought was better.

For a couple of months, we made dozens of trips to the neighborhood post office to ship boxes of books and other belongings to Nadya's sister, who stored them in her garage until we arrived and found a place to live. Finally, in early June 2013, we boarded a train to Krymsk for the 40-hour journey to start our life in South Russia. This completed the freshman and sophomore levels of my cross-cultural training. The junior and senior levels would be much more demanding.

# 9

# FIRST DAYS IN OUR NEW HOME

Geography wasn't the only thing that changed when we moved to South Russia. On the surface, Nadya and I experienced a slower pace of life than in St. Petersburg, but deeper issues arose. The main problem we faced at first was our normally strong communication broke down. Later, the emergence of politics as a major concern caused Nadya to lose friends while I experienced strong doses of Russian nationalism for the first time. Furthermore, we received the first indications of potential health problems for Nadya.

We arrived in Krymsk on a warm, sunny June afternoon. Built in a predominantly agricultural region, the city was dotted with small shops and markets, while in the part of town where we were staying, most people lived in small, modest houses with gardens in the back. Life there moved slower than in St. Petersburg. No crowds, no traffic jams, and no rush to buses. My main contribution to the cultural development of Krymsk happened at dinner one evening while we were enjoying locally grown corn-on-the-cob. Apparently, no one in Nadya's family had ever put butter on corn before because when my butter-laden knife slid across the juicy yellow kernels on the corn in my hand, everyone except Nadya looked at me like I was putting dog poop on it. Maybe out of loyalty as my wife, Nadya almost always tried the weird American things I ate, so she also put butter on her corn. It created a true picture of trust in marriage. Her sister and the rest of her family managed to put aside their disgust and tried it themselves. After taking a bite, they remarked it made the corn taste like movie-theater popcorn.

A few days later, Nadya and I boarded a bus to the first city on our list of possible language school locations, Novorossiysk, a city of about 240,000 on the Black Sea coast about 50 miles from Krymsk. However, because of the narrow, winding road the bus took over and around hills, it took almost two hours to get there. In a picturesque location between a line of hills on one side and the sea on the other, the city is a major Black Sea port and home to part of the Russian Navy's Black Sea fleet. We mainly toured the city on foot, making stops at the beach and a small park with a World War II exhibit about the Soviet defense of Novorossiysk against the Nazi invaders. In general, it was a nice place to visit, but we didn't notice a lot of vehicle traffic or people on the streets. As a result, we didn't think there was much potential for starting a school there.

A couple of days later, we traveled two hours (about 70 miles) by bus to the other city on our list, Krasnodar. The bus wasn't air-conditioned, and when we arrived in the late morning, the temperature was already 97°F. We already knew the city was much larger than Novorossiysk, with an official population of between 700,000 and 800,000, although we later learned from residents that the actual population was probably about 1 million. Krasnodar has many agriculture-related businesses as well as regional offices for many other companies. In addition, it is a pretty city, with lots of trees and parks and a nice walkway lining the Kuban River. Krasnodar's business activity seemed much larger than in Novorossiysk, which meant more potential for a school. We made our decision.

Another factor in Krasnodar's favor happened not long after we got off the bus. Despite having a city map, we were trying without much success to find a certain place. Nadya asked a woman on the sidewalk for directions. Asking such a question to someone on the street in St. Petersburg usually led to two possible responses: one, the person would ignore you and keep walking, or the person would say, *"Ne znayu"* ("I don't know") and rush off. Instead, this woman stopped, looked at the map, and apologetically said, "I'm sorry, I don't know." What's more, she stopped other passersby to ask them if they knew. I was astounded. Their behavior reminded me of people back in Kansas or Georgia. A few minutes of discussion passed before we determined where we needed to go. After everyone else went on their way, I asked Nadya, "Are you sure we're still in Russia? They were too nice." This and similar encounters in Krasnodar improved my overall image of how Russians react to strangers and how I generally looked at Russia. It no longer felt so cold, both in terms of weather and friendliness.

We rented a temporary apartment until we could find a location for our school and move closer to it. The red-brick apartment building was definitely a step down from where we had lived in St. Petersburg, but it was guarded by some friendly *babushkas* who were always sitting and talking on some benches near the entrance. There were also plenty of trees around to help block the South Russian sun.

The next job was going through all the red tape needed to start a new business in Russia. France may have invented bureaucracy, but Russia made it an art form. Poor Nadya had to face the bureaucrats alone. It wasn't easy. In one office, the clerk ridiculed her so much she left in tears. (A not uncommon result in Russian government offices.) Finally, after visits to eight offices, we were given a business permit under the name Campbell Language Center.

At the same time, we needed a location. In Russia, many apartment buildings have stores and offices on the ground level. Nadya found a vacant two-room office inside one apartment building, including tables, chairs, storage cabinets, and bookshelves. The rent was about as good as we could get. Sharing the bottom floor with us were a beauty salon, insurance agency, and a few other businesses I can't remember. The building was near a bus stop on a major east-west street in a neighborhood of about 100,000 people. With a population of that size, we figured we should attract students. A small grocery store was a short walk past more apartment buildings in the opposite direction from the bus stop. Nearby were additional stores and restaurants, including fruit and vegetable markets and a combination pizza/sushi restaurant. Even farther were a tram stop, another major street to cross, and a shopping center, which included a large grocery store and a Burger King.

We visited a printing company for finishing touches, where we chose a logo and ordered promotional flyers and two metal signs to advertise the school. After that, we placed the flyers in as many locations as we could. We also met people living in the nearby apartment buildings, especially those with children whose parents wanted them to take English lessons. In addition, Nadya contracted with someone to design a website for us. Our official start would be on September 1st, the official first day of school throughout Russia.

Nadya also started to advertise lessons online. After we were in Krasnodar for about a month, she got a call from a young college student looking for lessons from a native speaker. In St. Petersburg, it would have been no problem. I could get on the metro and be at her apartment in about 30 minutes, or vice versa. Krasnodar, however, has no subway, and the only public transportation besides trams were slow-moving buses or usually crammed minibuses called *marshrutkas*. Traffic jams on the narrow two-lane streets were almost constant, any time of day or night. She said it would take her between 90 minutes and two hours to reach our apartment. However, she was able to find a meeting room at the large library downtown about an hour from both of our apartments, and she became my first Krasnodar student.

Along with advertising the school and cleaning and arranging our office, we found an apartment in a 10- or 12-story building near the school. Apartment-hunting in Russia involves more than checking listings online. The biggest issue, Nadya said, is you usually have to go through an agent. The agent's fee, naturally, is added to your cost. As a result, finding an apartment takes time, patience, and prayer. Our apartment had two bedrooms, a bathroom, and a kitchen, but no common living area. We also rented out the other bedroom, but everyone who lived there stayed just a short time before moving on, so I don't remember much about them.

Nadya and I occasionally found time to explore our new city. Founded in 1793 on the banks of the Kuban River as a Cossack fortress to guard Russia's southern border against the Turks, the city was originally named Yekaterinodar ("Catherine's gift") after Empress Catherine the Great. Cossacks are a Slavic people group ranging from Ukraine to southern Russia once known for their horsemanship and military skill. They played a major role in defending the borders of the Russian Empire in tsarist times. Today, Cossacks present dance and musical shows downtown every weekend during the summer.

In the center of the city lies the old part of town where ornately designed brick or wooden homes or offices dating from the late 1800s or early 1900s line cobblestone or brick streets. Some of the major attractions are downtown along Ulitsa Krasnaya (which can be translated as "Red" or "Beautiful" Street), the city's main street. Plenty of stores, restaurants, and bars can be found on the street, which is closed off to traffic on weekends. The city also features parks, concert halls for a professional choir and orchestra, statues, and various other things to see and do. Shoppers can choose from a couple of big malls, and there are plenty of fast-food places. In addition, several universities are in Krasnodar, especially Kuban State Agrarian University, which was near where we lived. After being in Krasnodar for a while, I told Nadya Krasnodar reminded me of my birthplace of Rome, Georgia, and Wichita, Kansas, another city where I lived for several years. Both cities feature several universities and cultural attractions but still retain an agricultural and blue-collar feel.

September 1$^{st}$ finally arrived. Nadya had rounded up quite a few children for classes with her, but the demand from adults wanting English lessons was much less than we thought. In St. Petersburg, many students preferred native speaker teachers, and my schedule was so full that I sometimes had to turn prospective students away. I didn't have that problem in Krasnodar. Nadya and I found that the level of English instruction in Krasnodar schools was lower than in St. Petersburg schools. Most instruction focused almost solely on grammar and translation, not on communication. As a result, a student who would be classified as intermediate in English in St. Petersburg would be considered advanced in Krasnodar. I often would have one class in the morning and another in the evening, with nothing in between. As a result, I ended up teaching middle school and high school students a lot. For both years we were in Krasnodar, I led a group of middle and high school students two evenings a week. They were a fun group, even when they made me want to pull my remaining hair out.

I tried to find creative things to do with them. For example, I got the idea from an article to use movie or old radio scripts to practice conversation. Because of that, in class, we did the scene from *Titanic* where Rose wants to jump off the side of the ship and the witch scene from *Monty Python and the Holy Grail*. (The lone girl in the group had to be both Rose and the witch.) Our final year in Krasnodar ended with an open house for parents where we performed *The Hitch-Hiker*, a radio play first broadcast by Orson Welles in 1941. It pushed the students to the limits of both their knowledge of English and their introversion, but I think they liked doing it.

My experience with adult students was mixed. Many were like one man who contacted Nadya after seeing an ad mentioning me as a native speaker teacher. He told Nadya he had been looking for a native speaker teacher for a refresher course and wanted lessons with me. First, I gave him the English placement test all new students must take. After that, I had a general conversation with him to ask about his English background and goals for studying English. While we were talking, I asked him if he had ever visited an English-speaking country.

"Yes," he answered. His face was beaming. "I spent two weeks in England last year on business."

"Great," I exclaimed. "Did you practice your English while you were there?"

The expression on the man's face turned to horror. "Oh, no!"

"Why not? You were in England, the home of the English language."

"I was afraid if I made a mistake, they would think all Russians are stupid."

His response was the result of his own insecurities, but that fear was common among many Russians I met. He had his first lesson a few days later, but after talking for a while and having a quick grammar review, he said it was going to be harder than he had thought. He called in sick for his next lesson. When I asked him if he could make the lesson after that, he said he would call me. I'm still waiting for that call.

Not all my interactions with adult students were negative, however. I tried my Saturday afternoon history group again, and although it didn't attract as many participants as the St. Petersburg group, those who came were motivated to discuss. One of the most talkative members of the group was Oleg, a native of Kazakhstan, who offered many interesting insights. He said most Russians have someone in their family history who spent time in prison, which has led to a type of prison hierarchy and even prison vocabulary creeping into everyday Russian life. Another one of my favorites was a pediatrician named Alexei. Alexei told a story his grandparents had passed down about life during Stalin's forced famine (or Holodomor) of the 1930s, which affected Ukraine and southern Russia. Once, while militia patrols were scouring rural areas looking for anyone with food, a couple of officers stopped at their house.

"Your family looks very healthy," one of the officers told the grandmother. The men searched the farm, but they didn't find corn kernels the grandmother had wrapped in a tarpaulin and stuffed deep inside the well. The kernels were all the family had to eat.

Fewer students for me had a practical result—Nadya and I were making less money. We weren't in danger of being thrown out into the street, but our financial situation was much tighter than in St. Petersburg. The financial stress led to the most serious disagreement we had in our marriage.

We were walking along the river one afternoon a few months after we arrived in Krasnodar. We had just passed a small Russian Orthodox church when Nadya said we were barely clearing expenses and I needed more students.

"I'm not turning any away," I said. "In St. Petersburg, I never had any trouble finding students."

"So you think we should have stayed in St. Petersburg?" she asked.

I hesitated. "Maybe we should have."

"So you're putting this all on me?"

Nadya became angry at me. I didn't blame her. I should have made sure we explored everything thoroughly before we left St. Petersburg, but I let my naturally laid-back personality keep me from asking hard questions that I feared might derail Nadya's idea. We usually made decisions together, but in this case, my passivity left everything on her shoulders.

Nevertheless, our financial situation improved somewhat in a few months, mainly because many parents wanted their children to take English lessons in the afternoon and evening after school. As a result, Nadya hired three part-time teachers, and I ended up teaching a few classes for young people. As far as the discussion, Nadya and I moved past it with mutual forgiveness. More than once, we said it was an advantage we had been married before because we shared no romanticized view of marriage. We knew unpleasant things would come up, but we were committed to each other and wouldn't allow them to harm our relationship.

Another issue that confronted us was corruption. Corruption is a problem throughout Russia, where news reports often refer to the Russian government as a "kleptocracy." From what Nadya said, it's an attitude that permeates Russian society from top to bottom. According to a 2020 report from Transparency International, an organization working in more than 100 countries to end corruption, Russia ranked 128th out of 180 countries in the amount of corruption in the public sector.

In St. Petersburg, I met a number of students who had dealt with it first-hand. For example, one of my students was the director of a shipping company that exported and imported items between Russia and China. He estimated his company paid about $1.2 million in bribes each year to the government customs offices at the port of St. Petersburg. A common scenario, he said, occurred when a customs agent found a misspelling in a cargo manifest. He would inform the company he could not allow the item on the manifest to enter the country with the spelling error on the document. Instead of sending the product back to China, money directed to the right person would usually take care of the situation. Eventually, my student had a meeting with a high-level official in Putin's government, and the problem was solved.

In another case, a friend of a friend was attending a university in St. Petersburg. An exam was scheduled, but the other students in the class and the professor had worked out a deal where the students would pay the professor the equivalent of $100 and get a good grade. The student, however, insisted on taking the exam.

"Why?" the professor asked. "You won't even have to show up for class, and you'll get a good grade."

The student replied that she wanted to get the grade honestly. As a result, she and the professor sat in the classroom alone on exam day while she took the test.

Nadya and I saw more of that in Krasnodar. Two of my students attending Kuban State Agricultural University told us it was common for professors to seek bribes for tests. One professor informed students on the first day of class they would not get any grade that semester without a $100 bribe.

This practice even extended to the public school level. Some Russian-speaking teachers told us it was not unusual for the parents who wanted their children to attend a prestigious university to pay teachers or principals at the start of the school year to ensure their son or daughter got good grades. The parents of one of the students in my teen class must have been used to this. The student was intelligent, but he was always 30 minutes late to class for no reason, rarely participated in class, and never did homework. Whenever I questioned him about being late or failing to complete assignments, he just smiled. In time, I quit asking.

Nadya and I didn't have much time for anything but work. We found a Russian Baptist church we attended for a few months, but services were very formal, traditional, and long. One of the assistant pastors and his wife invited us to dinner one evening, however. They told us about their grandparents, all four Baptist pastors, who were arrested during Stalin's purges in the 1930s and sent to the Kolyma gulag above the Arctic Circle in the Soviet Far East. Only two returned. The other two were never heard from again. We next tried another church, but it turned out to be like an American megachurch, only in Russian. We became friends with a couple at that church, however. The wife told me she thought I was brave for coming to Russia. I told her I didn't feel particularly brave. Besides, I added, some people might call me crazy. She and her husband also asked which church or ministry was supporting us? My answer was none. Nadya and I were just a couple of Great Commission Christians, referring to Matthew 28:18-20: "Then Jesus came to them and said, 'All authority in heaven and on earth has been given to me. Therefore go and make disciples of all nations, baptizing them in the name of the Father and of the Son and of the Holy Spirit, and teaching them to obey everything I have commanded you. And surely I am with you always, to the very end of the age.'"

Tired of church shopping, Nadya and I decided to attempt something we had talked about before we got married to start our own church. One of our part-time teachers, named Kamila, told Nadya she was interested in learning the Bible and exploring Christianity, so we met every Sunday morning at the school for Bible reading and discussion. Kamila was always regular to attend and asked a lot of good questions. We finished each meeting with lunch. After that, Nadya and Kamila usually went shopping, leaving me with a free Sunday afternoon.

The year 2014 began with great news as Rita gave birth in January to a son, William, back in St. Petersburg. However, that was one of the few positive events to happen in the next year or so. Nadya's reactions to Russian political developments beginning that winter created a rift between her and some of her closest friends, and I encountered Russian nationalism at a level I had never experienced before. Most importantly, however, Nadya had to visit doctors about pain in her abdomen.

# 10

# THE RUSSIAN BEAR AWAKENS

The next month, the world spotlight focused on Krasnodar for at least one day as the city lay along the Olympic torch's path to Sochi, Russia, 180 miles to the south, site of the 2014 Winter Olympics. Krasnodar streets were lined with spectators one late morning as the torch procession wound through the city. Whether all of the crowd was there by choice was another question since two of my students who attended Kuban State Agrarian University told me they were required to be there on the threat of being given a failing grade if they weren't. I had no reason to doubt them.

Russia scored a huge propaganda victory with the Olympics. The Russian government poured billions and billions of dollars into construction and training for the Olympics and followed that up by staging an impressive high-tech opening ceremony and winning a record number of gold medals. I was standing in line at a bakery the morning after the opening ceremony. Two older women were in line ahead of me, talking about the opening ceremony. "The world now sees how advanced we are in technology," one of them said. During the competition, as Russia won another gold medal, two Russian women I knew were having a conversation online. "Our nation is getting stronger and stronger every day," one woman said. "We are invincible," the other replied.

The burst of nationalism provided by the Sochi Olympics was nothing compared to the reaction to the annexation of Crimea. The annexation took place in March 2014 following protests in Ukraine which deposed Ukrainian President Viktor Yanukovich and overthrew the Ukrainian government. Clashes between protesters and police led to 130 deaths. Ukraine had sought closer ties with the European Union, but Yanukovich was perceived as backing away from them. On February 22nd, the next-to-last day of the Olympics, Yanukovich fled to Russia. That same day, the Ukrainian parliament voted 328-0 to depose him. Russia considered the vote illegal and refused to recognize the interim Ukrainian government.

Protests erupted against the new Ukrainian government in parts of eastern and southern Ukraine. The controversy centered on the peninsula of Crimea in southern Ukraine, where 58 percent of the population is ethnic Russians. In a referendum in March, the residents of Crimea voted to integrate the area with the Russian Federation. However, many countries have not recognized the referendum because of many irregularities in the voting, including the presence of Russian troops before and during the election. At the same time, fighting broke out in an area in eastern Ukraine called Donbas, where the minority Russian-speaking population claimed they were suffering discrimination from the Ukrainian government. Although much of the world accused Russia of breaking international law, Russia charged the Central Intelligence Agency with instigating anti-Russian demonstrations in Kyiv and other parts of Ukraine. All of this was happening about 200 miles from Krasnodar. Spurred by non-stop coverage from Kremlin-controlled TV stations and websites, Russian nationalism was awakened.

Before moving to Krasnodar, I hadn't noticed much political activity in St. Petersburg. However, once Nadya and I moved to South Russia posters supporting Russian leader Vladimir Putin and his United Russia Party were almost everywhere. Rural areas, such as the Krasnodar region, were where Putin received much of his support.

The cry was heard and seen all over Russia in 2014, *Krim nash!* ("Our Crimea!"), the belief by the overwhelming majority of Russians that Crimea rightfully belonged to them rather than Ukraine. Heavy fighting was going on at the Donetsk airport in eastern Ukraine between the Ukrainian Army and a combination of Russian forces and separatists sympathetic to Russia. The tanks, equipment, and personnel had somehow appeared in eastern Ukraine despite denials by Putin and the Kremlin that Russia was involved in the conflict. There were many reports of "little green men," masked Russian soldiers wearing unmarked green uniforms and carrying Russian weapons and equipment. In one famous quote, Putin responded that any Russian soldiers in Ukraine were "on vacation" and not at their official duties. Russia, he continued, would no longer stand to be regarded as a second-rate power under United States domination. He told his domestic audience he would not stand for any more encroachments by the U.S. and NATO forces on Russia's borders. Any problems in Russia were caused by the West in general and the U.S. in particular. As a result, his approval rating among Russians soared to 80 percent or higher.

In Krasnodar, Nadya and I lived far enough from the front that we didn't see much evidence of the fighting. I read online about a few Russian tanks passing through the city, and early one morning, while waiting on a bus, I saw some military trucks heading out of town on the highway leading to Crimea. MiG fighter jets flew overhead a few times, but I don't know if the flights were part of routine training or related to the conflict.

The controversy affected us most in our teaching and Nadya's personal life. Children and teens were not immune to the constant stream of propaganda and extreme nationalism displayed on television and repeated by their parents and other adults. Photos and videos appeared of elementary-school students dressed in military gear and receiving lessons on using weapons. Once, Nadya said one of her students, an 8-year-boy, interrupted class to ask her, "Do you know what the Americans are doing in Ukraine?"

Annoyed, Nadya replied sharply, "No, and you don't either. Get back to work."

A 14-year-old boy who met with me for lessons every Monday evening for a few months told me after class once that he would not be able to make it to the next week's lesson because he was going to be at a camp instead. At the start of our class two weeks later, I asked him for details. He said he and most of the boys in his school were excused for a week to go to the camp, where they learned such skills as digging foxholes, throwing grenades, and disassembling and reassembling an AK-47 rifle. At night, they were taught about Russian "history and culture." On many warm spring mornings, I saw teen boys and girls dressed in white shirts and black pants marching in formation in front of a school near where we lived in Krasnodar. Some people I knew said that was common in Soviet times.

Adult students were also influenced. One woman told me in class, "I'm willing to pay any price, even poverty, to keep Crimea." It didn't matter to her that the Kremlin was diverting money meant for hospitals, schools, and pensions to pay for a new bridge to connect Russia with Crimea and make other improvements. Many other adults we knew also suddenly changed. They were still friendly, but any mention of Crimea, Ukraine, or Putin sent them into zombie mode where rational communication was difficult, if not impossible. About the time I left Russia, the government had begun organizing nationwide civil defense and war mobilization drills.

In the minds of many, war was imminent. One Sunday night, a Russian TV talk show featured supposed military analysts who predicted how fast Russian tanks could overrun Berlin and Paris and how long it would take for the Russian Navy to threaten Great Britain. A TV meteorologist devoted part of his weather forecast one evening to explain his prediction of what would happen if there was a thermonuclear blast over Nebraska.

Nadya, however, was more disturbed by the situation than I was. Her deep sense of justice kicked in. She spoke out against Putin's rigged election in Crimea and the *Anschluss* in eastern Ukraine from the start. In addition, she was in contact with many Ukrainian organizations supporting their troops against the Russians and their Ukrainian allies. Several times Nadya asked me if I minded donating money to supply helmets and other equipment to the Ukrainian military. Because of this, Nadya had constant disagreements with some of her family and many of her friends and acquaintances. Some of them considered her a traitor and cut off contact with her.

A couple of factors, I believe, help explain the reactions I saw from many Russians. Unfortunately, sometimes it didn't seem like the American government had a clue about either one.

The first dates back to the late 1980s and early 1990s. Almost overnight, the Berlin Wall fell, communist governments in countries from East Germany to Romania and Bulgaria to Estonia disintegrated, and the Soviet Union collapsed. To Western eyes, the Cold War was over, and a bright future of democracy and free enterprise seemed to lay ahead for Eastern Europe and Russia. With no more Cold War between East and West, American leaders thought, the "peace dividend" could allow funds to be diverted from the military and intelligence to other needs. Russia at the time had a pro-Western president, Boris Yeltsin, who in turn had a second-in-command named Vladimir Putin. Although a former KGB officer, Putin seemed to have a lot of progressive ideas.

While the 1990s were economic boom times in the U.S., they were the opposite in Russia. The Russian economy lay in shambles, the military was weak, and millions of ordinary Russians lost everything after the devaluation of the ruble. The low price of oil and natural gas — Russia's only major exports — added to the financial misery. Political instability led to a military coup attempt against Yeltsin, which was thwarted. The Russian Mafia stepped in to fill the power vacuum. An American English teacher I knew in St. Petersburg who was living in Moscow at the time said it was almost like the Wild West. Once, he had to hide under his seat on a train he was riding when a gunfight broke out.

Russia, meanwhile, tumbled from its position in world affairs. A conflict with Islamic radicals broke out in Chechnya, and, in Russian eyes, the U.S. and NATO reneged on several agreements, including establishing bases close to the Russian border and failing to provide economic assistance to Russia.

In 2000, Putin was elected as Yeltsin's successor. At first, he instituted some seemingly democratic reforms in government, but they didn't last long. However, he and Russia benefited from the worldwide rise in oil prices in the early 2000s. The Russian economy and the number of jobs grew, while Russians became more intertwined with the world banking and investment sector. The upper one percent with lots of rubles to spare began investing some of them in Western Europe, the U.S., or anonymous offshore accounts, especially in Malta.

As some of my Russian friends told me, the early Putin years were the best economic times in Russian history. In addition, Putin has used a lot of that revenue to rebuild Russia's armed forces. While the U.S. military was sent to fight Islamic terrorists in Afghanistan and Iraq, Russia revamped its naval, air, and ground forces. They seemed to be particularly proud of the newest generation of the T-90 Armata tank, at least from what I read. You could even see young mothers pushing their babies in buggies shaped like a T-90 tank, complete with markings and insignia. In addition, I knew more than a few Russian men who spent a lot of evenings playing online tank wargames. Putin also announced the completion of what he called an "invincible" hypersonic missile system supposedly capable of traveling at speeds of over 3,836 mph and able to avoid detection. Constant malfunctions with Russian mechanical systems make you wonder how effective they would be in actual combat, but I prefer not to underestimate anyone.

The second factor goes back a lot farther. Around 1524, Philotheus, a Russian Orthodox monk serving in a monastery in the city of Pskov, announced the entire Latin (Catholic) world was sinful and the "first" Rome and the "second Rome" (Constantinople, now Istanbul) had fallen into heresy and ceased to be the centers of the Christian world. The center of the Christian world would now fall to the "third Rome," Moscow. "For two Romes have fallen, a third stands, and a fourth there will not be," his prophecy stated. From this came the belief among many Russians that their country has a special role in defending true Christianity against the error and decadence of the West.

Almost 500 years later, the Third Rome idea still has plenty of adherents in Russia. An online image I saw early in my stay in Russia carried a headline across the top: "Russia – Hope of the World." In the center was a large photo of a Russian Navy destroyer with helicopters flying above and a rocket taking off. In the background were photos of Putin, Patriarch Kirill of the Russian Orthodox Church, Russian Foreign Minister Sergei Lavrov, and two other people I couldn't identify. Farther in the background was a photo of a Russian Orthodox chapel, while behind it was a faint drawing of a representation of Jesus' face taken from an icon. Underneath the photo in tiny letters was a portion of Matthew 5:9: "Blessed are the peacemakers...."

This philosophy has led Russians to see themselves as the saviors of neighboring countries, if not all of Europe. Many Russians will tell you that their nation has saved Europe twice—in 1812 against Napoleon and 1945 against Hitler. Russia also sees itself as "big brother" and "protector" to Slavic nations in Eastern Europe and the Balkans. Serbia has long been a staunch ally of Russia, but many in other nations such as Ukraine, Poland, and the Baltic countries of Estonia, Latvia, and Lithuania don't look back to Soviet occupation and domination with glee. In recent years, pro-Soviet monuments in many Eastern European countries have been torn down.

In addition, the Kremlin projects Russia as the protector of what it calls "the Russian world," pockets of ethnic Russians living in other countries, especially those bordering Russia. Many of these

136

ethnic Russians were moved to other countries around the time of World War II to replace residents who were forcibly removed from their homes and shipped by rail to labor camps in the Ural Mountains of Siberia. Conflicts have definitely risen between, for example, ethnic Latvians and Russians inside Latvia. I witnessed a small but vicious exchange once on a bus in Riga, the capital city of Latvia, when I was there to get a new visa from the Russian embassy. Two middle-aged women, one Latvian and the other Russian, got into an argument over "freedom."

"There is nothing more important to me than freedom," the Latvian said.

"You won't say that when you're hungry," the Russian replied with a sneer. "What is freedom? An illusion." Of course, not all Russians think like that, but I heard similar statements more than once.

Since the fall of the USSR and the independence of the former Soviet republics, and the withdrawal of Soviet forces from Eastern Europe, the Kremlin has sought to look after the "rights" of Russians living in those countries. One of the main ways is to insist on the right of students from Russian families to be instructed at school in the language spoken at home, usually Russian. Ironically, it's a right Central Asians and other immigrants and people groups living in Russia are often denied. In addition, the Kremlin broadcasts pro-Russian news to Eastern Europe over the radio, T.V., and the Internet to influence the opinion of Russians living there.

From my research, as early as 2008, Putin met with military, intelligence, and other leaders to devise a strategy to allow Russia, as Putin said, "to rise from its knees." Its immediate goal was to return Crimea to Russia, establish a pro-Kremlin government in Ukraine, and strengthen ties with "the Russian world." Its ultimate goal was, and I believe still is, to create a multipolar world where the United States is no longer the dominant superpower, drive a wedge in NATO and the Atlantic alliance between the U.S. and Europe that has existed since World War II, and replace that with a Eurasian partnership between Europe and Russia.

I experienced some of the reaction of the Russian public to this even while I was in Krasnodar. One of my students told me he thought it was only "natural" that Europe and Russia would be aligned. My response was he was overlooking about 400 years of political and social history between Europe and North America.

In short, the Russian strategy was a continuation of Soviet intelligence activities dating back to the 1920s called "active measures." With a former KGB officer at the head of Russia, it's all very plausible. Among possible active measures are disinformation and propaganda, ranging to more violent means such as assassination and political repression.

As part of this hybrid warfare, a disinformation and propaganda campaign began to influence the world, especially Western and U.S. opinion. The Kremlin diverted millions of dollars for education, hospitals, and pensions into funding such media outlets as Russia Today (now R.T.) and Sputnik. The role of the state-sponsored media is to create content advancing Russian narratives, advance political narratives against Russian opponents, and sow conspiracies undermining trust in democracy. In addition, the government created the Internet Research Agency, with headquarters in St. Petersburg just a couple of metro stops from the apartment where Nadya and I lived after we returned to the city in 2015. The agency hired hundreds of employees with at least some knowledge of English to work at what became known as the "troll farm." They aimed to infiltrate social media using false names and fake accounts to disseminate propaganda and discredit political leaders seen as hostile to Russian interests and advance those seen as friendly to Russia. Unlike the Cold War days when Soviet propaganda sought to extol the virtues of Marxism over capitalism, the new Russian propaganda sought to undermine not only democracy but also the entire idea of objective truth.

Often when I would give evidence for my opinion to a Russian listener, the response was, "Well, that's your truth." From a Christian perspective, in my opinion, the Russian strategy doesn't seem far removed from the serpent with Eve in the Garden.

Being a stickler for the truth but still not aware yet of the scope of what we were facing, in mid-2014, I joined some other Westerners and Eastern Europeans either living in the West or still in their home countries who got on RT, Sputnik, and Facebook to counter the propaganda and false posts we read. You could call us trolls, too. I became a sort of "rock star" among my colleagues since I lived in Russia and could counter false claims about conditions there. Some of the pro-Russian posters were out of their league because of their poor English, but others were more fluent in English and had been carefully coached on what to say. To deal with people like that, I had to do my homework. In addition, there were plenty of pro-Russia Westerners online who saw Russia through rose-colored glasses and were always ready to magnify the West's faults, especially anything negative about the U.S. They were the kind of people Lenin or Stalin referred to as "useful idiots."

Gradually, many of my friends and I saw the futility of us going up against what we learned early on was a Russian government behemoth. The source of the frustration came from the fact Western nations were doing little or nothing in response. President Barack Obama instituted sanctions against Russia and drew some lines in the sand, which Russia ignored, but the American government seemed to be doing little about influencing world opinion in favor of the West. I even emailed my congressman at the time, a Kansas Republican, telling her that from my position overseas, it seemed like the U.S. and the West were losing the information war. I never got a response. We often reported trolls and fake accounts to Facebook, but we were generally ignored. For every fake account or page Facebook removed, thousands more were left. More than that, however, I had a life away from the Internet.

To me, one particularly troubling aspect of the Third Rome philosophy is that it has at least partially led to a certain chauvinism in some Russians. "They think they are special," a Ukrainian friend told me. One YouTube video Nadya showed me was of a sixth-grade teacher in Russia telling her students that Russians are the only people in the world with the cognitive ability to see relationships between events. A number of Russian "scholars" have examined purported ties between the intellectuals and philosophers of ancient Greece and Russia to the point of one writer calling Russians "northern Greeks." Other "scholars" point to supposed links from Sanskrit and ancient Indian culture to Russia. As far as I know, neither Greece nor India has acknowledged those ties. Russian TV and politicians reinforce that feeling of superiority. These are a couple of examples: One TV show I watched, for example, called the Arctic Ocean a "Russian sea." Another example was where Vladimir Medinsky, Russia's culture minister, was quoted in a May 2014 interview as saying Russia's perseverance through the last century was proof that "our people have an extra chromosome." Perhaps you have to experience it to understand, but, in my opinion, this Russian hyper-nationalism goes beyond any American exceptionalism.

This is a little bit of a tangent, but a related piece of Russian culture I observed was how important it was to appear strong and show no weakness. An example was President Obama. While Obama experienced a lot of popularity in many countries, he was extremely unpopular in Russia. A lot of that deals with sanctions and some of his social policies, but to many Russians, what they saw as his vacillations were a sign of weakness. Caricatures of Obama's face appeared in Russian urinals, American flags with Obama's photo were dragged behind buses, and Obama became the butt of countless jokes on Russian TV comedy shows.

Words like "compromise" and "admitting fault" were anathema to more than a few Russians I met. I often heard that Russians respect a strong enemy over a weak friend. For instance, I had a student for a short time who was director of the Krasnodar branch of a French-based vegetable processing company, similar to Green Giant. He told me he and many other Russians respected Ronald Reagan as president—despite his "evil empire" quote about the Soviet Union, which many Russians still resent—because of his firmness as a leader. "With Republican presidents, we know what to expect," the director said. "We can't predict what Democratic presidents will do."

Finally, nowhere is Russian nationalism as evident as in the belief of the "deep Russian soul." Writers and observers from Dostoevsky and Tolstoy to the present have used untold gallons of ink writing about the supposedly mysterious Russian soul. Answers are all over the board. I read and read and listened and listened and observed and observed and tried to get an inkling of it for myself. I even asked a couple of students I had become friends with, "What is this 'deep Russian soul?'" They just laughed. I started figuring Russia out soon after I arrived in St. Petersburg and had developed my own ideas on the subject. I wanted confirmation, however, so I emailed a close friend of mine who is Russian and pastors an evangelical church near St. Petersburg. My one-line message was, "What is this deep Russian soul thing?"

His simple answer came back, "Romans 1." The first chapter of the book of Romans from the Bible.

My quick response was, "That's what I thought." The deep soul of all mankind without Christ.

With all of that going on, in Spring 2014, Nadya started getting sharp pains in her abdomen. She visited two doctors, who found cysts on her ovaries. Both said surgery would not be needed. Instead, all she needed to do was change her diet. That seemed to be the default cure for many Russian doctors. When I told my student

Alexei, the pediatrician, about my allergies, for example, his reply was, "Have you tried changing your diet?"

I laughed and answered, "I don't eat through my nose." He knew I was kidding.

Nadya's condition was no laughing matter, however. She seemed to improve somewhat, but every once in a while, the stabbing pains returned. Matters reached a crisis point when we visited St. Petersburg over the Christmas and New Year's holidays.

# 11

# HEALTH MATTERS AND RETURN TO ST. PETERSBURG

Under Russian law, Russian residents are entitled to free health care under Obligatory Medical Insurance. Employers can also offer additional Voluntary Medical Insurance. The wealthy few can afford to go to private hospitals. At such places, patient care is excellent. Everyone else goes to public hospitals, where conditions can range from ideal to unsatisfactory. I visited the inside of three such hospitals while in Russia, one in Krasnodar and two in St. Petersburg. Their exteriors were made of red brick and looked a lot like American schools from the 1960s. Interiors were generally dark, with walls often painted institutional green. There were none of the soft colors and cheery decorations found in Western hospitals and clinics. I never observed it myself, but I saw photos from some Russian hospitals showing such issues as greenish liquid coming from restroom pipes and collapsing ceilings in patient rooms. I also never saw a private room. During Nadya's hospital stays, she shared rooms with up to five other women.

I had three doctors as students while in Russia, including Alexei, the pediatrician. All seemed to be very caring and professional. However, Russian physicians receive unbelievably low salaries, some around the equivalent of $200 a week. (Many public-school teachers earn about the same amount.) As a result, many top Russian doctors leave the country to practice in Europe, North America, or Australia for much higher pay. While many Russian medical professionals sacrifice financial reward to serve people, there are also at least a few unqualified doctors. One example Nadya told me was of a woman she knew in Nizhnevartovsk who took her son to the hospital late one night when he was suffering from splitting headaches. The doctor in the emergency room gave him a cursory examination and told the mother to give him some aspirin. The mother and son returned home, but his severe pain continued. An hour or two later, he was dead. I told Nadya that would have been a certain malpractice case in the U.S., but she said it was nothing in Russia.

Unfortunately, that wasn't the only medical horror story I heard in Russia. For example, Russian "bedside manner" is quite a bit different than in the West. When she was in labor with Rita, Nadya said the doctor and nurses (nurses have even fewer qualifications and earn less than physicians) screamed and cursed at her. Apparently, from what she said, that is normal in Russian delivery rooms. Shortly before I returned to the U.S., a video that went around Russia showed a doctor at a Siberian hospital beating up a man in the hospital waiting area. The man died, and the doctor was arrested, probably only because the incident was on video. Prior to the Sochi Olympics, doctors and nurses from other parts of the world were flown in to train Russian medical staff on proper courtesy and care for patients.

Finding an ambulance was another adventure, at least in Krasnodar. There, the average wait for an ambulance was about two hours. One person in Krasnodar told Nadya and me that he called for an ambulance when his elderly mother became seriously ill. It took a couple of hours for the ambulance to arrive, but the mother died in the meantime. What did the ambulance crew do when they arrived at the scene? Curse at the man for not canceling the call. Instead of depending on an ambulance, many Krasnodar residents take a taxi to the hospital. I became sick with a flu or virus in Krasnodar once, and Nadya had to call a taxi to take us to the hospital. I didn't have to stay overnight, however.

In December 2014, Nadya and I flew from Krasnodar to St. Petersburg to see Rita and our nearly one-year-old grandson William over the New Year's holiday. One morning while we were there, Nadya was overcome by excruciating pain. I felt helpless as I had never seen her in so much agony. Fortunately, the ambulance service in St. Petersburg was much better than in Krasnodar, and she was soon transported to a nearby hospital. The problem was the cysts on her ovaries again. The St. Petersburg surgeon asked Nadya why the doctors in Krasnodar hadn't removed them? Nadya didn't know, but she told the surgeon I asked the same question at the time. Even though surgery removed the cysts, the surgeon said they would return.

Not long after the surgery, we decided we would move back to St. Petersburg at the end of the academic year in May. Medical care was a significant factor, but also *babushka* Nadya wanted to be closer to Rita and William. In addition, since many Krasnodar residents didn't want lessons from a native speaker, I was still bringing in only a fraction of the income I had earned in St. Petersburg.

Nadya and I made another major decision. Because of Russia's deteriorating political and economic situation, we would finally get Nadya's visa to live in the U.S. as my wife. We had done preliminary work on it earlier, but a number of factors kept us from making much progress. First, I was required to have a long-term Russian visa, which I didn't qualify for until a change in a visa agreement between the U.S. and Russia in 2013. Second, there was a mountain of paperwork mainly Nadya had to compile, which took a lot of time.

After getting back to St. Petersburg, the first step we had to take was to travel to the U.S. embassy in Moscow to submit a form at the U.S. embassy containing documentation showing we were a legitimately married couple. Part of the reason is American immigration officials want to cut down on the number of international marriages where the spouse from another country weds a U.S. citizen only to get a green card. We sent the embassy signed affidavits from friends, photos of us together, airplane and train tickets with both our names on them, and, of course, our wedding documents, all translated into English and sealed. Because we had been married for longer than three years, our requirements were actually less stringent than for newlyweds. Then there was the $425 fee. As of Summer 2021, the fee had increased to $595. All of this documentation had to be approved before Nadya could even apply for her visa.

Meanwhile, life in St. Petersburg resumed as before. We lived in the same apartment as Rita, her husband, Tim, and William on the fifth floor of a 19th-century apartment building in the center of the city. The apartment consisted of three bedrooms, a kitchen, a small closet with a toilet, a bathroom, and a shower. Rita and Tim slept in one bedroom, Nadya and I in another, and William in the third bedroom. Some gas-light and candle fixtures remained on the walls, which made me imagine what the old apartment had seen in its lifetime. Nearby were two metro stations, a large shopping mall, plenty of shops and grocery stores, and a variety of restaurants. Some of the city's major historical and tourist attractions were a 15- to 30-minute walk away down Nevsky Prospekt. Across the street from our building was a park with a statue of famed 19th-century Russian poet Alexander Pushkin. Tourists interested in Russian literature sometimes took photos of the statue or even left flowers on the anniversary of his birth in 1799 or his death in 1837 when he was mortally wounded in a duel. Older people used the park to sit on benches and reminisce while children used it as a playground. Beer cans and vodka bottles often found on the grass in the mornings left evidence other activities took place at night. Family and friends were glad to see us again, as well as directors at the schools where we had worked in the past. It didn't take long for students to schedule lessons with me.

Some of my most interesting students came along during my second stay in St. Petersburg. To meet one of my most unique students, you had to exit the metro at one particular station, take the two-minute ride up the escalator, and turn right at the exit. You would then pass a building with a Subway sandwich shop, a bank, and several other stores. After crossing a busy street, turn right again and pass more stores and a police training center before crossing another street. To the left stood a three-story building with a bar and a Chinese restaurant on the first floor, a couple of business offices on the second floor, and on the third floor, one of the language schools where I taught. There, I encountered Yuri.

Short and slender, Yuri was in his late 20s or early 30s, had sandy blonde hair, and worked in a hardware store. He said he attended the school's conversation groups to improve his English-speaking abilities. What I recall most about him, however, is his answers often came from both his heart and off the wall. On one evening, about ten adults were sitting around a conference-room table giving good yet predictable responses to the question from their workbook: "Describe a time in your life that you wish you could relive." Soon it became Yuri's turn to speak.

He said his memorable event happened when he was 11 or 12 years old, and he and a girl in her late teens went camping together at a lake. The details grew juicier: "We got drunk, and she gave me some of her drugs. Then we had sex. The next day, we walked to the other side of the lake, where people who were like hippies were staying. We drank some more and smoked some of their marijuana. I would like to do that again."

How to respond to an answer like that was one of many situations my TEFL training didn't cover, so I simply said, "Interesting. Your vocabulary is quite good." A few students laughed, others softly giggled, and another man gave him a high-five.

Russians are generally more reserved than Americans, but once Russians open up, they sometimes tell you more than you want to know, either in groups or in one-on-one conversations. One of my students worked for Sberbank, the largest bank in Russia, and took private lessons from me for a few months to improve her English for her job. One time, a question in her textbook asked, "Name an obstacle that you have overcome in your life." It didn't take her long to come up with an answer: "When my husband and I were first married, and our children were young, I had an affair with a married man," she admitted in a matter-of-fact tone. "It nearly tore our family apart."

A man in one group at another language school told a similar story. He asked the meaning of the word "date," as when a man and woman go out together before they are married. I knew he was a newlywed, so I smiled and said, "Of course, you can only date your wife now."

"No," he answered with a serious expression on his face, "I also date other women."

Another man spoke up. "Sure, what's wrong with that?" he asked.

All I could do was shrug.

Another example of marital harmony came when I asked a class what they did over the New Year's holiday. One man said, "My wife and I went to the village we come from."

"That sounds nice," I replied. When I first arrived in Russia, I would have imagined a cozy scene of a family gathered around the fireplace. However, by this time, I had been in the country long enough to know better.

"Not really," the student said. "I got bored and returned to St. Petersburg. I went to parties and drinking with my friends."

"What did your wife do?"

"She stayed there until she got bored. Then she came home."

Admittedly, those kinds of revealing answers were rare, and as far as I could tell, most Russian married couples I knew were living happy lives together. But these responses served as a welcome diversion from such usual topics as verb tenses, articles ("a," "an," and "the"), and the finer points of English vocabulary and usage. A lot of the problems students had resulted from translating directly from Russian to English or English to Russian, never a good idea, but some originated from the human desire to reach a goal with as little effort as possible. For instance, once a student asked me for tips on how to learn new vocabulary.

"One of the best ways is to find articles online about subjects you're interested in, then read them," I told her.

"You mean I find articles in Russian and then translate them to English?" she asked.

"No, I mean read articles in English."

"But I won't know a lot of the words."

I was trying not to laugh. "That's the whole idea. But there's this amazing new invention called a dictionary. They come either online or in a retro print edition. You can find lots of words there."

She tilted her head in disbelief. Her shoulders drooped. A whine came through her voice. "That's hard."

I shrugged and answered: "Life is hard."

One change we made from our first time in St. Petersburg was we started attending a church closer to our apartment. Katerina, my former student, attended there before she moved to Spain while we were in India and recommended it to us. The pastor was named Jon, a North Dakota native who worked as an electrical lineman before getting the call to preach. He was learning Russian and even survived the process of becoming a Russian citizen. His wife, Larisa, came from Belarus, and they had a young daughter. Nadya often interpreted Jon's messages, and I think Jon liked having an American male friend he could talk to about anything from faith to football.

While classes proceeded, Nadya and I felt pressure from the rampant nationalism combined with political and financial turmoil. Sanctions placed against Russia by Western countries and against some foreign products by Putin's government increased prices and dramatically dropped the ruble's value. When I arrived in Russia in

December 2010, the exchange rate was 28 rubles for 1 U.S. dollar. By late 2015 and into 2016, the exchange rate for the ruble plummeted to 85 rubles for one dollar. One of my students, a wealthy rail line owner, told me he lost $1 million in one day in currency exchange. For students, that meant English classes with foreign teachers, such as me, became much more expensive because we were paid at a higher rate than native Russian speakers. I began experiencing a drop-off in the number of people wanting lessons. It wasn't dramatic but noticeable.

Nadya, meanwhile, continued to crusade for justice. She spoke out online against Russian activities in Ukraine and Putin's policies in general. She also attended a few opposition meetings in St. Petersburg. "If you get arrested and sent to the gulag," I told her half-jokingly, "you won't get your visa."

Another related event happened to someone we knew about this time, which pointed to how serious the situation had become. The church where Nadya and I had our Christian wedding ceremony was the location of an English movie night every Tuesday. Most evenings, activities consisted of food, table or card games, followed by an English-language film or TV program with subtitles. After watching the show, the leader, an American missionary, led a discussion in English. Because it was a church-sponsored program, many questions related to ethics, morality, or some philosophical issue. Usually, 10 to 20 people were there. Nadya and I attended two or three times, and it was fun.

One afternoon when we were in our apartment, Nadya asked me to watch a video with her on her laptop. The video was of a "news" report from *TB Zvezda* ("TV Star"), a national television station operated by the Russian military. In the report, a crew showed up at a movie night and tried to interview the missionary. The report said the missionary was a former American Army officer who used the free pizza offered at movie nights to recruit participants to spy for the U.S. It also showed interviews with people claiming they had attended movie nights before and testified they were recruited to be American spies. The only word to describe the report was "ridiculous." The missionary was never in the military, and movie night organizers and regulars said they had never seen any of the people interviewed. What's more, even though incomes in Russia are generally lower than in the U.S., a few slices of pizza wouldn't be enough to entice many Russians to commit treason. Nevertheless, about a week or two later, the missionary received a letter from the Russian government saying he, his wife, and their two children had three days to leave Russia. They were deported.

I told Nadya someone in the group must have informed authorities to focus on this particular movie night. Many other English movie nights sponsored by language schools and churches in St. Petersburg continued with no resistance. Along with threats to pull the plug on the Internet in Russia, nostalgia for the Soviet Union, and laws aimed at limiting freedoms theoretically guaranteed under the Russian constitution — it was a small part of what I called USSR 2.0.

For me, the constant barrage of nationalistic propaganda, the illogical and often contradictory regulations, and what I felt like was general craziness finally got to me. The last straw happened one afternoon in the kitchen when a school I taught classes for announced a new policy I considered idiotic. I can't remember the details, but it set me off. I spent at least 10 minutes releasing five years of pent-up frustrations in a loud tone of voice I usually didn't use. Nadya stood up, smiled, put her arm around my neck, and said, "Right now, I love you more than ever. Now you see what we Russians have to deal with our whole lives."

Around this time, Nadya and I had another serious talk. She told me after observing what was happening in Russia, the way the Russian government treated its own people and its neighboring countries, and how the overwhelming majority of Russians supported the government's actions, she said she thought I had always shown real strength.

"You can turn the other cheek, ignore insults, and give gentle answers," she said. "That is the way to be strong." She also apologized for some things she had said to me in the past that she thought had hurt me.

There was no need to apologize, I replied. Within my first few months in St. Peterburg, I detected many cultural differences between Russians and Americans, and I recognized where I would need to adapt. In addition, I told her even though we strove to be citizens of the Kingdom of God before citizens of our countries, we still carry the background of growing up in two different cultures.

"You were right when you said I needed to get a thicker skin and take things less personally," I concluded, "but I know there are things I do that drive you crazy."

I honestly didn't think she needed to apologize, but the fact she said it made me feel beyond loved.

We also got some good immigration news. A few months after we returned to St. Petersburg, we heard from the embassy that our documents certifying us as a legitimate married couple were approved. This was a huge miracle because we were legally married in the eyes of the U.S. government, and Nadya could apply for her spouse visa. It also meant the U.S. would lawfully recognize our marriage, so we wouldn't need another wedding ceremony.

However, another mountain of paperwork lay ahead. Nadya had to compile a seemingly endless list of papers basically documenting everything in her life. By Spring 2016, we had received all the documents. All we needed to do was schedule Nadya's required interview at the embassy in Moscow and make an appointment for Nadya to have a required medical checkup at a certain clinic near the embassy. Oh, and pay the visa fee, which at the time was $325. By summer of 2021, the fee had increased to $535. I once figured with the visa, spouse verification, and other documents, airfare, and expenses after we arrived in the U.S., the total price tag would have been $4,000 to $5,000.

Most Americans, however, have no idea about the cost and red tape of immigrating to the U.S. More than one friend asked me, "Can't you just get Nadya a plane ticket since she's your wife?"

My answer was, "I wish."

One question remained: When could we go to Moscow for Nadya's visa interview? Her gynecologist said cysts were reappearing on Nadya's ovaries and recommended a hysterectomy to take care of the problem once and for all. Nadya and I discussed whether she should have the surgery before leaving for the U.S. or after we arrive. I told her although American medicine was excellent, it was also expensive. The gynecologist said the surgery would be routine, so I suggested having it in Russia before leaving the country. Nadya scheduled her surgery for June 22nd and the visa interview for July 8th, her birthday. We thought two weeks should give her enough time to recover from the operation before making the trip to Moscow.

# 12

# THE DAYS THE EARTH
# STOOD STILL

The days leading up to Nadya's surgery passed uneventful-ly. She went to the hospital early in the morning of June 22nd, a Wednesday, and had surgery that afternoon. I was working for most of that time. I wasn't allowed to see her immediately after the operation, but before she left for the hospital, Nadya told me to call her that night. I phoned after my regular Wednesday night adult conversation group, but she was still woozy from anesthesia. This made talking to her difficult, but I managed to understand I could see her around lunchtime the next afternoon.

When I arrived after my normal Thursday morning lesson, she was lying in bed, with a happy grin lighting up her face. Her smiles always made me happy, and her hug felt warm. Her room was rectangular with beige walls and overhead lights hanging from the ceiling that looked like they had been taken from the elementary schools I attended in the 1960s. There were five beds with a small wooden nightstand sitting next to each. At the time, Nadya and another woman were the only patients sharing the room.

Nadya told me she would have to remain in the hospital for a week (Russian hospitals keep patients a lot longer than American hospitals). Most importantly, she told me what food and other things from the apartment to bring her later. She had warned me before about inedible Russian hospital food, so I knew what to expect. We talked for about an hour about nothing important before I needed to leave to prepare for my evening classes. Besides, she began to yawn and looked a little tired. Before I walked out the door, I gave her another hug and kiss and reminded her, "I love you."

As often happened, Rita, Tim, and William were staying at the dacha outside St. Petersburg, so I had the apartment to myself. I would miss having Nadya around for a week, but the thought consoled me that soon, Nadya would have her visa, and we would be on our way to the U.S. The selfish part of me, however, was looking forward to a week of peace and quiet. That evening, I took the metro to an Internet Technology company on the east side of St. Petersburg, where I taught classes every Tuesday and Thursday night. Early the next morning, I rode the metro and a bus to an oil company office on the south edge of St. Petersburg for a weekly 8 a.m. Friday class. Nothing happened out of the ordinary, and I got back to the apartment about 10:30. I piddled around for about an hour until I thought I would see what was in the kitchen for lunch and then visit Nadya.

I was about to leave my room when a knock came at the door. It was Rita with Tim and William. Since it was a Friday morning, my first thought was they were planning to spend the weekend at the apartment. William walked in, saying in toddler Russian, *Baba Nada* (*Babushka Nadya* or "Grandma Nadya"). I told him, "*Baba Nada* is still at the hospital." Rita and Tim looked at each other. Their narrow eyes and tense lips told me something was wrong.

"Harold," Rita said, pointing toward mine and Nadya's bedroom. "Go, sit."

I sat in the chair next to my desk while Rita sat in another chair. Tim and William stood. Rita looked me in the eyes and gulped. "Mama died," she said.

The apartment was on the fifth floor, but I felt like I had fallen to the basement. I couldn't breathe. I didn't have time to think because there was another knock on the door before I could say anything. It was Rita's mother-in-law. Right away, we walked the 15 or 20 minutes from the apartment to the hospital, although in my mental and emotional state, I didn't remember a step I took. When we reached the hospital, Rita and her mother-in-law went inside to talk to the doctor and other hospital staff while I waited outside. Everything was in Russian, so I was pretty much out of the loop from this point on.

A few minutes later, Rita returned with the wedding ring and other jewelry Nadya wore and gave them to me. Rita explained the best she could in English that, according to the other woman in the room, about 6 p.m. the evening before Nadya tried to get out of bed to use the bathroom. As she was putting on her slippers, she stood. When she was completely upright, she collapsed back onto the bed, shook a few times, and died. An autopsy later that night showed she had a blood clot that started in her leg but went to her heart and lungs when she stood up. The doctor and the coroner said the blood clot probably came loose during her surgery. Rita was listed as her mother's emergency contact because she was a native Russian speaker and could communicate with hospital staff.

I was then taken across a courtyard separating the hospital and the morgue to complete more paperwork. Mostly, what I wanted to do was see Nadya's body to prove to myself that she was no longer alive. I told Rita I would like to see the body as that is a custom in the U.S. for closure. She asked the man at the desk, but he answered, "No." Anger and frustration boiled inside. I didn't want to take "no" for an answer, but there was nothing I could do about it at that point. Count it as one of the complications of living in a different country with a different language and customs. I was still the visiting team in the white jersey, just like at the wedding. With their work at the morgue finished, Rita and her mother-in-law walked back to the hospital to take care of more business.

Meanwhile, I stood outside in the courtyard, praying and trying to hold myself together. I called Jon, the pastor of our church. He and his wife and daughter were on the way to their country home when I blurted out the news the best I could. They came back to town and gave me the name of a restaurant where we could meet for dinner that evening and talk. I next called Vitaly, the pastor who performed our church wedding, and told him what happened. By that time, it was 1:30 in the afternoon, and I decided to go home. Again, I don't know how I made it. All I knew was I needed to tell somebody, so I could release the emotional volcano erupting inside me.

Fortunately, before politics took it over, Facebook was a good place to connect with friends and family. I posted what happened and received a lot of encouragement from everyone. A little later, Rita returned to the apartment and said the funeral would be Monday morning. I contacted all my students and schools, told them what happened, and canceled my remaining classes.

That evening I took the metro to the restaurant to meet Jon and Larisa. They said they would have a service for Nadya at church Sunday morning, and they had already invited Rita. I considered this the actual funeral because it matched what Nadya would have wanted. I also told them the man at the morgue said I couldn't see Nadya's body before the funeral Monday morning. At that moment, seeing her body became my top priority. Perhaps it was because that gave me something tangible to focus on while so many other half-formed, indescribable thoughts were swirling inside my head. Jon called a common friend, Tim, a Ukrainian who spoke both Russian and English at a native level, and asked if he could accompany me to the morgue the next morning to see if he could convince someone to let me see her. Without hesitation, he agreed.

Tim met me at the apartment the next morning. I was prepared to do things the Russian way, so I took the equivalent of about $100 in case I needed it for "payment." When we reached the morgue, Tim explained to the man working there it was common in the U.S. for the family to see the body before the funeral. I told him I needed only one minute. He remained silent but took a few steps to open to door to the room where the bodies of Nadya and four men were being prepared for burial. Nadya lay on a gurney, draped in a white sheet covering all of her except her neck and head. Her face looked as peaceful as if she were sleeping next to me in our apartment. As I promised, I only needed to look at her face to see this was a nightmare come true. The man didn't give any hint he expected money, so I simply thanked him and walked away.

That afternoon, Rita, William, Tim, Tim's parents and grandmother, and probably a half-dozen other people crowded into the apartment. I stood by silently, listening to all the chatter but understanding little. I really wanted to be alone and insulate myself with peace and quiet. However, that wasn't to be the case, as a short time later, Nadya's mother, Nina, arrived by train from South Russia and came to the apartment. Tears streamed down her face as she wept and sobbed uncontrollably. I honestly don't remember anything else that happened that day.

The next morning, Rita and her friend Zhanna took the 10-minute walk with me from the apartment to Jon's church. With plenty of piercings and tattoos, Zhanna was another punk. She was also fluent in English and would provide me with a lot of translating and interpreting over the next few days. More than that, Zhanna said Nadya always treated her with respect, unlike the reaction she usually got from others. My thinking was still hazy, so I don't remember much about the service except Jon said it was the only funeral he had ever conducted in Russia where he knew for certain the eternal destination of the deceased. He also thanked Nadya for interpreting many of his messages from English to Russian and for the encouraging emails she often sent him. Rita and I were next given a chance to speak. All I remember is I told Rita we could get through the next few days on emotion and adrenaline, but the hard part would come after that when the everyday routine resumed. The rest of the congregation also shared their thoughts and memories of Nadya.

Monday, the day of the funeral, was one of the strangest days of my life. Along with Rita, Tim and William, and Rita's in-laws, I arrived at the morgue shortly before 9 a.m., when the funeral was scheduled to start. More than two dozen people were standing outside, waiting for the door to be unlocked. I knew a few of them, especially Vitaly and my friends and former students Michael and Nastya. I also couldn't help but notice three middle-aged women roaming through the crowd, weeping and wailing and causing a racket. Like the open sewers in Bareilly I had only read about before seeing them in person, these must be paid mourners, I thought. Ironically, the open sewers and the paid mourners seemed to be filled with the same substance. Maybe it was my journalist instinct or more likely emotional self-protection, but before the funeral started, I slipped into an observer role. I was there in person, but I felt like I was watching everything on video. I was missing Nadya more than I could describe, yet I knew beyond a doubt she was safe in a much better place.

Eventually, someone unlocked the door, and everyone entered. Inside the dark, spartan room sat five open wooden caskets containing the bodies of the deceased persons I had seen Saturday morning. Each casket was painted black. Nadya's casket was at the far end of the room. I estimated about 20 or 30 people had gathered around. Zhanna was standing next to me to interpret.

Nina insisted on a Russian Orthodox funeral. Nadya was dressed in a white gown with a lace covering over her head and a cardboard band around her forehead with writing in Old Slavonic, the Russian Orthodox worship language similar to Latin for Roman Catholic services. I couldn't read the writing, but many headbands in Orthodox funerals say, "Holy God, Holy Mighty, Holy Immortal, have mercy on us." Flowers lined the inside of the casket, with a small icon of Jesus and the Virgin Mary sitting on top of Nadya. I knew Nadya well enough that if she could look down on us, other than the flowers, she would have hated the whole thing. She never liked elaborate productions, especially when they were focused on her.

As the weepers wailed, someone handed out candles. In addition to interpreting from Russian to English, Zhanna also told me what to do next and in which hand I should hold the candle during different parts of the service. Even more so than at the wedding, I again felt like the visiting team wearing the white uniform.

A few minutes later, a priest entered wearing black vestments and carrying a censer filled with incense. For about 10 minutes, he spoke and chanted many words and phrases that Zhanna said she couldn't interpret into English. Smoke from the censer covered Nadya's body with a cloud as many in the crowd bowed with their lit candles and repeated certain sentences and phrases after him. Without saying anything else, the priest walked out of the room.

Many then stood around, weeping and sobbing. Vitaly read some verses from the Russian Bible off his cell phone; then, people lined up to walk around Nadya's casket. Some of them were almost hysterical with grief. Although I had already shed many tears and would shed many more, I found myself in the unusual position of comforting and consoling people at my own wife's funeral. After most of them had viewed Nadya, I went up to her. I mouthed, "I love you, but I'll see you later," and bent over to kiss her forehead. It felt like kissing cold marble.

"She's not there," Vitaly said.

"I know," I answered. "But it was my last chance to do that."

A few more minutes passed until two men came to attach the lid to the top of the casket. The lid was also painted black, with a white Orthodox cross displayed on top. The men next carried the casket to a blue passenger bus parked outside. Someone opened the rear door to allow them to slide the casket inside and attach it securely to the floor. Zhanna told me the family could ride in the bus to the cemetery while others would go in their own cars.

I sat in the back of the bus next to Nadya's casket. Nina sat across from me, bent over the casket and wailing without ceasing. I felt like no one but the Lord knew I was there, yet I didn't care. As we drove through the city, I tried to focus on Revelation 21:4: "He will wipe every tear from their eyes. There will be no more death or mourning or crying or pain, for the old order of things has passed away." My mind also repeatedly played back two old hymns, "There is a Fountain" and "What a Day That Will Be." Outside, it may have looked like I was under control, but inside, I possessed the strength of a wet noodle.

After driving through more traffic, we reached the outskirts of town. The bus turned off the four-lane road we had been taking onto a narrow two-lane street. In five or ten more minutes, we reached the cemetery entrance. The huge cemetery was covered by a network of dirt roads passing through the burial plots. I had never seen anything like it. Instead of well-manicured lawns, tombstones were lined up almost next to each other while grass and weeds were high enough to cover some of the markers. The bus traveled along one of the dirt roads for quite a while, driving past trees, tombstones, and occasional piles of trash lying on the ground. Finally, at the intersection of two roads, we reached the gravesite.

Next to where the bus parked was a dumpster full of dead flowers. Piled close to the dumpster was a mound of food wrappers, plastic bottles, paper, and other trash. A backhoe and three cemetery workers stood next to a hill of freshly dug dirt a short distance from the grave. Drivers of the cars following us were finding places to park. In total, there might have been 20 people gathered.

The rear door to the bus opened, and the same men who put Nadya's casket in the bus carried it to a small metal table someone had placed in the middle of the road. One of the men opened the lid to the casket, and more crying ensued. Fortunately, the paid mourners didn't show up at the grave. At first, most people were just standing around. Nina continued wailing. I don't know everything she said, but she told Vitaly something bad about me. Vitaly later told me he had no idea what she was talking about. In the meantime, the bus drove away.

Vitaly read some more scripture and said a few words in Russian. He wasn't part of the funeral plans; he took it all upon himself. The men then closed the lid again, and with the help of the cemetery workers, lowered the casket into the grave. Following that, a cemetery employee took a plastic bucket and filled it with dirt. I stood at a distance, waiting to see what would happen. As the worker held the bucket, each person took three handfuls of dirt and threw them onto the casket, one handful at a time, reminiscent of Genesis 3:19 in the Bible: "By the sweat of your brow you will eat your food until you return to the ground, since from it you were taken; for dust you are and to dust you will return." I was one of the last people to take part in the scene. Throwing that dirt was one of the hardest things I have ever had to do. I can't explain why, but it left me with a creepy feeling that remains whenever I recall it.

When the service ended, people brought food out of their cars. Guess where they placed food, along with plates and containers? Right, on the metal table that held the casket. A woman asked me if I would like something to eat, but I politely declined. For one thing, it was only 10:45 in the morning. Even more than that, I didn't want to eat anything off the surface of where Nadya's earthly remains had sat for the last time.

Jon was standing next to his van, which he parked near where the bus had been. "Heartless, isn't it?" he asked. All I could do was sigh and nod my head. I talked with him for a while, then spoke with a few other friends, especially Michael and Nastya. There is an old Russian saying that if you ever make friends with a Russian, you are friends for life. With Michael and Nastya, that is certainly true.

It's mostly a blur now, but not long after that, I got back to the city with Tim, Rita, and William in their car. Along with Zhanna and a few other friends of Rita and Tim, we went grocery shopping for Rita and Tim. They would be staying at the apartment for a while, and, as vegetarians, they needed some healthy foods. Nina would also be staying there.

I enjoyed having someone with me right after the funeral, but I still needed a little time alone. While the young people were doing something in the apartment, I told them I was going for a walk. I hadn't eaten since breakfast, and about 15 minutes later, I ended up at one of our neighborhood McDonald's. After I sat at a booth with my tray of a Big Mac, *kartofel* ("fries"), and a Coca-Cola *standart* ("regular"), I looked up toward the ceiling. I knew Nadya was up there, with her arms crossed and eyes rolling while letting a big sigh. She always hated me eating fast food and drinking any kind of soft drink because she thought they were unhealthy. "If you die before me," she told me with a fake frown more than once, "I'll kill you."

That day, I smiled and whispered, "You're not here now, sweetie, and I need some comfort food."

While I was sitting there, I decided my time in Russia was over. If I had stayed, everything would have reminded me of Nadya. What's more, she wouldn't have been there to support me. I felt like my right arm had been yanked out of my body. When I told my friends and family back in the U.S. that I was returning, everyone was happy, but no one was surprised. However, a few obstacles remained for me to overcome.

# 13

# LAST DAYS IN RUSSIA

Nadya's funeral took place during White Nights, the period from mid-May to mid-July when daylight in St. Petersburg extends long beyond midnight. While tourists and locals walked the sidewalks lining the city's maze of rivers and canals, ate and drank at outdoor cafes, or sat on park benches until late into the night, for me, the six weeks between the funeral in late June and my return to the United States in early August passed in a gray fog.

It took about a week for my brain to clear enough to think. Even then, I could focus for only a few minutes before another round of tears gushed like a Yellowstone geyser. Staying busy might help, I decided, so I started gathering Nadya's things. The first item I wanted to set aside to keep was the CD-ROM of our wedding. The last time I noticed, it was under a certain book on a lower shelf in the bookcase in our room. Still, when I looked, nothing was there except a few specks of dust. Where could it have disappeared? I had seen it in that exact place before. Panic flooded my fragile mind. My breathing grew faster. I sat on the floor and stared at the bookcase. Is this what a mental breakdown feels like? I closed my eyes, took a deep breath, and exhaled. A few more tears welled in my eyes. All I found the strength to do was tilt my head toward the ceiling. "Jesus," I thought, "I'm not leaving Russia without our wedding video."

In less than a minute, my breathing slowed, and part of the cloud shrouding my brain dissipated. An impression came to me to look under a book on the highest shelf, a place where I hadn't thought to look. I stood and lifted the book off the shelf. The CD-ROM was sitting there. I smiled, shook my head, and mumbled, "Thank you." Later, I remembered Nadya told me she had moved some of our things to keep them out of the reach of our toddler grandson, William, but she didn't tell me where she had put them.

One afternoon around that time, I was sitting on the floor in my room going through more things while Nadya's mother, Nina, was in the kitchen. Without knocking, she entered the room and placed a piece of paper at my feet. On the paper, she had written in English, "100,000 rubles," roughly $2,000 at the time.

*"Shto eta?"* ("What's this?") I asked her in Russian.

"It is custom in Russia to take care of family," she answered in English. Her English skills were limited, so I knew she had rehearsed her line more than once before repeating it to me. Some of her past words also made it obvious she didn't think I was part of her family, a fact that, honestly, didn't bother me.

*"Ne yest."* ("I don't have it.")

Her eyes narrowed, and her lips twitched into an angry stare. Seconds later, she stormed back to the kitchen.

What now, I asked myself? First, my wife dies, and now my mother-in-law wants money. A few weeks earlier, Nadya closed out our bank account and exchanged the rubles for dollars to take with us to the U.S. The cash sat inside a large envelope I placed in one of my desk drawers. After Nina left the room, I couldn't think at first. One trick to survival in Russia I learned, however, was to discard any naivete and determine the worst-possible action another person could take. As a result, I didn't put it past her to enter my room while I was gone, find the money, and keep it. When Rita, Tim, and William returned from the dacha soon after that, I told them what had happened. Rita and Tim became angry, and Tim called his parents. They invited Nina to spend the rest of her time in St. Petersburg at the dacha with them. After she was gone, we hid the money in Rita and Tim's room, just in case. I never saw my mother-in-law again.

Except for those crises, I spent most of the time deciding which things were going back to the U.S. with me and which were staying. I left Nadya's clothes for Rita. However, our room was full of English textbooks, workbooks, and worksheets Nadya used while teaching. There was no way they could fit in my suitcase or carry-on bag, so I decided to donate them to the three main language schools we worked with. While it kept me occupied, leafing through the pages brought back a combination of happiness and pain. Every sheet and every book aroused a bittersweet memory, but like being pulled by a magnet, I felt drawn to look at each one. Over a week or so, I carried boxes of books and papers from the apartment and delivered them to the schools. The administrators and instructors were shocked at what happened but offered to help me in any way they could.

The most difficult job I had to do, however, was to teach one more class. Right after Nadya died, I canceled all my remaining private lessons and the classes I taught through schools. Yet, one of Nadya's students had paid for three more lessons, and he insisted on taking them. He was a native of the country of Georgia who bought used American and other foreign cars in eastern Europe and resold them in the St. Petersburg area. Normally, he had English grammar lessons with Nadya, but occasionally he practiced his conversation with me. When he arrived at the apartment for his first lesson one evening soon after the funeral, I greeted him with a friendly hello, but underneath, my heart wasn't in it. We sat at the kitchen table where Nadya used to help him with English articles, prepositions, verb tenses, and all the other grammatical issues which normally give native Russian-speakers trouble. This time, all I had to do was listen and correct his pronunciation. Yet, my mind kept picturing Nadya teaching there instead of me. A few times when I spoke, I had to clear my throat to choke back tears. Although he seemed satisfied with our conversation, I couldn't keep Nadya out of my mind. The hour felt like an eternity to me. I confess I was relieved when he texted a few days later to cancel his last two classes because he had to travel to Romania and Poland on business.

Other activities also kept me occupied. One day I accompanied Rita to three or four governmental offices to get death certificates and other documents in Russian for her and official English translations for me in case I needed them. Her friend Zhanna, who had interpreted for me at the funeral, also came along, mainly to guide me through the bureaucratic maze we were traversing.

A few days later, the ninth day after the funeral, Rita, Tim, William, and I traveled to the cemetery to place flowers on Nadya's grave. In Orthodox and Russian tradition, the ninth and fortieth days after a death have special significance to the deceased person's soul moving to its final resting place. However, many Russians now mainly think of these specific days as special times to visit their loved one's gravesite. As this was a custom I had never experienced, I reverted to my observer mode other than letting William arrange my flowers on the plot. As I stood there, I thought this might be the last time I would see her grave. I had to let go of her a little bit more. The feeling wasn't painless.

Still, the idea of the "last time" stuck with me. I didn't know when or if I would ever return to St. Petersburg, so I decided to visit as many places I had experienced as possible. I started with the major tourist attractions such as the Winter Palace and the Peter and Paul Fortress. While walking the streets of the historic district, I bought souvenirs to take back to give to my family and stopped to listen to the classical, folk, and pop melodies from the street musicians for a little bit longer than usual.

Next, I got on the metro to revisit the old neighborhoods where Nadya and I once lived. I started with the high-rise apartment building where we stayed for the first three months of our marriage. Nearby sat the grocery store where the cashier threw the change at me that winter evening soon after I arrived in St. Petersburg. If the same thing happened to me now, I thought with a smile, instead of being shocked as I was then, I would probably just laugh. Another day, I rode the metro to the Khrushchev building on the opposite end of the city, where Nadya and I shared a tiny apartment with people from so many countries. Walking from the metro station through the park, past the park benches where *babushkas* gossiped and working men swigged beer, and past the small, algae-filled pond where residents swam past midnight on warm White Nights helped relieve my stress, at least for a few minutes. My final "last trip" took me to the third neighborhood where we lived. For the final time, I admired the architecture and artwork inside the Avtovo metro station. From there, I took the 15-minute walk to our former apartment complex and then strode a couple of minutes more to my real destination, the grocery store where I often bought *shashlik*, similar to shish kebab in the U.S. Fortunately, the store had some in the deli section, and I took a package home for dinner. It served as more comfort food. My little tour might sound crazy to some, but in addition to bringing back memories, it provided some closure.

I also took a few out-of-town trips. Michael and Nastya drove me to Kronstadt, a city on an island in the Gulf of Finland at the entrance to the port of St. Petersburg and the last on my list of historic places outside of St. Petersburg I wanted to visit. It is now home to the Russian Navy Baltic fleet and the site of many stately churches, forts, and other buildings. Finally, I treated myself to a trip on the high-speed train from St. Petersburg to Moscow to visit Larry and Josie, the missionary couple we became good friends with when they lived in St. Petersburg but who later moved to Moscow. The time together strengthened me but traveling at 150 mph over the rails, I had only one question: Why can't the U.S. have something like this?

My trips make it sound like I was on vacation, but the fun times spent outside the apartment were the exception. The cloud overhead never completely went away. Waves of grief overwhelmed me at unpredictable times and places. I often tried to mask my emotions with smiles and platitudes, but the phony feeling I had inside made me stop even trying to cover up what I was feeling. Sometimes anger hit me. Not anger at God, but anger at Russian medicine for not detecting Nadya's blood clot. How could something like that cause the death of a healthy woman just two weeks short of her 44th birthday? Who had become a vegetarian two or three years earlier, didn't drink or smoke, and exercised regularly? It helped some when I learned about 100,000 Americans die each year from undetected blood clots.

At the time of my divorce in the mid-1990s, a popular song came out by Christian singer Pam Thum entitled, "Life is Hard (God is Good)." The lyrics described me. If I tried to read my Bible, I could barely read a page before my concentration shut down. I found I did better by listening to audio. If I tried to pray, no words came out. I sat in silence and remembered some of the bedrock principles of my entire life as a Christ-follower. One of the foremost that came to mind was, "A bruised reed he will not break, and a smoldering wick he will not snuff out" (Matthew 12:20).

The song concluded by describing that Jesus never promised a problem-free life, but He would be with us when life became hard, and He understood what we were going through. I was glad someone understood even when words escaped me.

One last thing to do was make reservations for my return to the U.S. My pastor friend Jon helped me book the flight for the second week in August. I spent my remaining days in St. Petersburg, finishing my "last things" list, packing, and saying goodbyes to Rita and the family. Sadness shrouded my last time with Rita, Tim, and William. I didn't know when I would ever see them again, and I was leaving behind my last connection with Nadya.

The day came to leave. The taxi taking me to Pulkovo airport just south of St. Petersburg came around 2:30 a.m. for my 5:55 a.m. Lufthansa flight to Frankfurt, Germany, the first leg of my trip home. Traffic was almost non-existent at that time of the morning, and we arrived at the airport in less than half an hour. Check-in went smoothly, despite the fact my suitcase weighed two pounds over the 50-pound limit. The friendly airline clerk at the counter waived off any extra charge. At passport control, my next stop, the face of the immigration officer who stamped my passport even revealed a slight smile. That was unusual enough, but his tone of voice when he told me, *"Do svidaniya"* sounded like he somehow knew it would be a long time, if ever, before I returned.

The sun was already over the horizon when the plane lifted off the runway. My final "last thing" in St. Petersburg was to look down from the early-morning sky on the city where I had spent much of the previous five and a half years. Memories of familiar landmarks, friends, former students and colleagues, and everyday life flashed through my mind. Living in a city with such rich history and culture had been a privilege. It was too early in the day to think about anything deeper than that, however, plus the flight attendants were bringing out breakfast. I ate while the plane skirted the Baltic coast, crossed Poland, and flew over Germany. As we descended before reaching the Frankfurt airport, cars and trucks were speeding on the *autobahn* below. The trip was one-third over.

I had a three-hour layover in Frankfurt before my United flight to Newark. I walked through the terminal, checking out shops and looking for a place to get something to drink, mainly to stay awake. Besides, I could say I had set foot in Germany. My next flight took off on time. Once the plane was in the air, my lack of sleep from the night before and all that happened in the past six weeks caught up with me. I slept for about an hour. My brain fog from St. Petersburg was still with me, so the rest of the flight passed in a blur. A few hours later, the plane descended over Manhattan, and we landed at Newark. Passport control went faster than expected, but as soon as I exited, I saw that my flight to Kansas City and dozens of other flights had been canceled. Hundreds of other passengers were also stranded, scrambling to reschedule itineraries. Two days passed before I finally made it to Kansas City thanks to more canceled flights and airline scheduling problems. Welcome back to the United States.

I wasn't on American soil long before I realized the country, and myself, weren't the same as when I left.

# 14

# LEARNING THE NEW ME

The experiences gained from living five years in Russia and five months in India followed me to the U.S. For the time being, I was living with my father and sister in the Kansas suburbs of Kansas City. The neighborhood consisted of typical middle-class homes, well-manicured lawns, and usually at least one sport utility vehicle parked in the driveway. If you walked down the sidewalk, anyone cutting the grass or watering the yard would say, "Hello," accompanied by a friendly smile. The cold St. Petersburg faces crammed inside metro cars at rush hour or the Bareilly women squatting in the dirt, forming cow manure into patties for heating seemed like a different world.

For a short time, I went through reverse culture shock, where I found myself having to readjust to what had once been familiar. I observed this almost 20 years earlier when a doctor and his wife I knew returned to the U.S. after serving as medical missionaries in Africa. Their teenage daughter reacted to the drastic change in her life by constantly criticizing this country and begging to return to Africa. Fortunately, my case wasn't as severe. Instead, my eyes were opened to how newcomers from other countries, bringing their own cultural backgrounds, could be perplexed by life here. The open friendliness of many Americans could be misinterpreted by a reserved Russian, while someone from a poor area of India could feel lost in a wealthy American suburb. The humbling part is any negative observations could well be true.

An example of reverse culture shock happened when I was taking a walk one morning. A young man and woman walking their dog were coming toward me from the opposite direction. As we drew closer, I moved to the edge of the sidewalk, but the man and woman stepped onto the grass to let me go past. The woman grinned and said, "Sorry!" The couple and the dog continued their walk, but I immediately thought about Nadya's reaction in St. Petersburg the afternoon when she and I met the woman with the dog and I got off the path to let them pass. I was able to contain myself from laughing, but I looked skyward with a smile and said, "See?" I imagined Nadya responding with the fake frown she always showed the rare times I was right, but she didn't want to admit it.

Overall, however, grief overshadowed everything I did, from renewing my driver's license to finding a job. Before I left Russia, my Uncle Charles in Cedartown, Georgia, a city of 9,000 about 60 miles northwest of Atlanta, told my father I could move in with him and be his caretaker as he was going blind and deaf. I thanked him but said I would prefer to find a job first to get my feet back on the ground in the U.S. About a month after my arrival, a friend and former colleague who worked as an assistant editor at the *Salina Journal*, a daily newspaper in Salina, Kansas, said there was an education reporter opening there and asked if I was interested. I was, and I ended up getting the job.

I moved to Salina, a city of 47,000 in north-central Kansas, in early September. My work performance wasn't poor, but my mind wasn't in my job. My concentration suffered. My memory seemed to vanish. I made silly mistakes. I felt mentally drained most of the time. Away from the office, I could be an emotional wreck. Without warning, memories and feelings of sorrow overwhelmed me like a tsunami.

For some reason, that often happened to me at the grocery store. One afternoon, I was walking down the juice aisle at Dillon's, a large supermarket chain in that part of the country, when out of the blue, a gigantic wave of sadness engulfed me. Somewhere near the plastic bottles of V-8 and Ocean Spray cranberry juice, my breathing grew heavier. Tears welled in my eyes. I had to stop my cart and regain my composure. No one else was standing in the aisle, so I don't think anybody noticed. If they did, they probably thought I was going nuts. I would have agreed. That was the first of quite a few "grief attacks" I experienced at grocery stores within the first year or two of Nadya's death. I never figured out, however, why so many occurred at supermarkets.

Although I was able to make friends, I nevertheless felt isolated and alone. That was nobody's fault, but perhaps it was my defense mechanism to keep more pain away. Maybe some people, not knowing how to handle someone with a recent loss, were keeping their distance from me. I needed help. Fortunately, it came.

At the church I attended, I was friends with a surgeon, Steve, his wife, Annie, and their two young sons. Annie's mother died a short time before, and Annie was still grieving her death. Under her leadership, the church became part of GriefShare, a network of thousands of grief recovery support groups around the world. Another group was forming at the church, and I signed up.

One of the first pages in the group workbook contained a list of more than 150 common responses to the death of a loved one, ranging from depression to fatigue to irritability to questioning your sanity. I checked probably half of them. One of the benefits of joining the group, however, was being with people who were wrestling with the same struggles. For the first time since Nadya died, I met people who understood the pain and stress I was undergoing.

I could only go to a few meetings because about a month before, I decided to take my uncle up on his offer to move back to Georgia to live with him. The main reason was the *Journal* and several more Kansas newspapers were sold to a nationwide media group known for buying newspapers and then downsizing personnel. I had already been laid off twice in my career, and I didn't want it to happen again. Along with that, I determined I wasn't cut out for 21st-century journalism, and I left newspaper work behind.

Along with my belongings, grief also accompanied me to Georgia. I wasn't as weepy as when I first got back from Russia, but the deep pain inside remained. June 23, 2017 — about seven weeks after I moved and the first anniversary of Nadya's death — was an especially tough day. The memories of what happened the year before were fresh. Inside my mind, I replayed every scene in an endless reel. I tried to pray that morning, but no words came, so I let the Holy Spirit pray for me. I posted on Facebook and received some encouraging messages, which helped. I also sent an email to Rita, who was mourning the loss of her mother. She sent me a photo of her, Tim, William, and their new son, Robert, placing flowers on Nadya's grave. Seeing that helped me feel closer to both Nadya and the rest of the family.

While I was dealing with those memories, life with my uncle turned out to be more difficult than expected. His eyesight and hearing were deteriorating, but he also showed signs of dementia, especially auditory and visual hallucinations. For a few hours in the middle of the day, he was lucid, but at other times his mood could change from calm to hostile for no reason. I helped him sign checks to pay bills and a few other things around the house, but he refused whenever I suggested going somewhere or doing something together. His day was spent lying on his bed, listening to the radio or the television with the sound turned up full blast.

His condition worsened. Paranoid his neighbors wanted to kill him, he kept three pistols in his room. When I later cleaned and went through everything in the house, I discovered two of them were loaded. I had already told my father that Uncle Charles's condition was more serious than was originally thought, and he needed professional care. One Saturday night, he telephoned the police from his room in the back of the house without my knowledge while I was in the living room. The police officer who knocked on the front door asked if I had called, and I said it was probably my uncle. As I was talking with the policeman on the front porch, my uncle came into the living room with a gun in his hand. The policeman persuaded him to put down the gun, but more officers were called to talk with him before he calmed down and returned to bed. I told my father about it, and he drove from Kansas City to check on him. While he was there, my uncle hallucinated that someone was on the front porch with a machine gun and other people were out to kill him. After that, a judge issued an order for him to be committed to a care center for treatment. He was transported to a hospital in Rome, Georgia, 20 miles north, for a week before being admitted to a Cedartown care center.

He seemed to be improving, but three weeks later, a nurse at the center called me to say he had stopped breathing. Paramedics tried to resuscitate him, but he died. His funeral was a few days later. All of this happened within my first six months of living in Cedartown. Although I wasn't close to him, the stress of dealing with his condition combined with my grief over Nadya and adjusting to life in a new location was almost overwhelming.

About six months later, a nearby church advertised it was offering a GriefShare group. I needed the encouragement because some of the same emotions and thought patterns that I had in Kansas were coming back. Fortunately, this time I could take the entire 13-week course, and, again, having new friends in the same situation helped give me a lot of support. What struck me at this point was realizing my "old normal" was gone and would never return. According to the course, the mind of someone who has experienced the trauma of losing a loved one is rewired. As a result, my responses to different situations may not be the same as they were before Nadya died. On the good side, I have found that I don't care what people think of me as much as I once did. On the negative side, however, I let little things bother me than before. It's frustrating, but I'm still in the process of learning the new me.

In addition to the effects of Nadya's death, Russia also followed me to the South in some ways. On one of my first days in Cedartown, I was using my laptop at the public library to take advantage of the free Wi-Fi. A young woman who looked to be in her late teens or early 20s sat at a table across from me, opened her laptop, and logged on to Skype. After she began speaking, I couldn't help but notice Russian words and phrases coming from her mouth. "No way," I thought, considering the unlikely possibility of anyone speaking Russian in small-town Northwest Georgia.

After the conversation ended, I walked up to her and asked, *"Izvinite! Ty govorish po russki?"* ("Sorry, do you speak Russian?")

Her eyes and mouth both opened wide. She told me she hadn't expected anyone else in the library to understand her and apologized for speaking loudly. I assured her she didn't disturb me. It turned out she was Ukrainian and a student at Kennesaw State University in Kennesaw, Georgia.

One of the first similarities I noticed between the South and Russia after I arrived in St. Petersburg was how quickly many Southerners and many Russians become defensive if they believe their region or their country is being criticized. Say something critical about the region's accent, food, or history, or bring up a stereotype such as cars sitting on blocks with a washing machine on the front porch to a Southerner, and you're likely to raise some hackles. Likewise, Russians seemed especially sensitive to stereotypes such as bears drinking vodka while playing folk songs on a *balalaika*, although some have turned them into jokes or cartoons.

Even in Russia, I encountered the image of the South, especially after the Ukraine situation erupted in early 2014. For example, some of the Confederacy's biggest fans now live in Russia. In St. Petersburg, someone placed Confederate flag stickers on metro car doors, and I once saw a Russian-language novel for sale in a bookstore about a group of Red Army soldiers transported by time machine from World War II to Gettysburg in July 1863 to help Robert E. Lee and the Army of Northern Virginia defeat Union forces. A number of Confederate (and Union) Civil War re-enacting units have sprung up in Russia. There was a photo online of Confederate re-enactors in Siberia drilling in the snow. I even became a rock star when I joined an American Civil War group on the Russian equivalent of Facebook and posted I was from the South and had distant ancestors who fought for the Confederacy.

I'm sure this is spurred more by modern anti-Americanism than by love for the Southland, and there is, unfortunately, a racist aspect. I quit the Civil War page because many of the comments were racist, and then there was the infamous Halloween party in Krasnodar. One of Nadya's students in Krasnodar invited us to attend a Halloween celebration in a spacious banquet hall near the bus and train station. Halloween is a relatively new holiday in Russia, where older people tend to dislike it because they consider it an "American" celebration. Still, increasing numbers of young people participate in it, mainly with parties.

Some of the party-goers to this event wore costumes, including a young man clad in an authentic-looking Ku Klux Klan outfit, complete with a white robe and hood and a noose tucked under a belt around his waist. However, what unnerved me most was his smile and the laughs of many of the others at the party. My skin crawled, and the hairs stood on the back of my neck. I leaned forward and whispered to Nadya, "Back in America, that guy would probably be killed." Nadya and I didn't stay long.

One more similarity between the South and Russia I observed was tradition, especially concerning a brand of Christianity that is often based more on the prevailing culture than the Gospel.

To many Russians, however, their country is morally superior to the Western world. I heard more than one Russian say something like, "Russia is more spiritual than the United States." On the surface, it makes sense. Russian Orthodox cathedrals are found seemingly everywhere, sometimes within a few blocks of each other in larger cities. Putin himself lights candles in church services while publicly speaking out against homosexuality and immorality. I saw many young people in their 20s or 30s stop and bow in front of statues of Christ or saints lining the outside of some church buildings as they walked past.

Statistics, however, show things aren't always what they seem. A survey published while I was in Russia said attendance at Russian Orthodox churches each week was about 8 percent. I can attest that the St. Petersburg metro was nearly deserted on Sunday mornings. The same survey indicated less than 5 percent of those identifying as Russian Orthodox actually believed Orthodox doctrine. For many, it appears, as long as they wear the cross they received when they were baptized into the church as a baby, how they live afterward doesn't matter.

After all this, I have to conclude I don't have all the answers. But that doesn't bother me.

Something I am certain of is what I told a friend when he asked me soon after I returned to the U.S., "If you knew what was going to happen, would you have still gone to Russia?"

Without hesitation, I answered, "Without a doubt."

That doesn't mean I don't have any regrets, however. At times, I disappointed Nadya. She usually didn't say anything, but occasionally I saw it in her face. I could have listened better, talked with her more, been more supportive of her. I could have been less busy preparing for classes or simply messing around. But there were so many other things. All I could afford when we got married was a simple golden wedding band Russian women commonly wear. I planned to surprise her with a diamond ring after she got her visa and we moved to the U.S. There were also places here in the U.S. such as Savannah, Charleston, and the Great Smoky Mountains I wanted to show her. For a long time after my return, I cringed whenever I imagined us in any of those locations. It took me a while to get up the courage to visit them myself. I regarded my trips there as "therapy."

Much more than that, however, I am convinced knowing Nadya for eight years and being married to her for five and a half of those years was more of a blessing than I can imagine. In that time, I experienced love and learned how to both accept it and give it. She listened to me and respected me. She restored my confidence in myself. I told her more than once that no matter what I was thinking about, my thoughts always returned to her. For some reason, even though she was way out of my league, she loved me. Nothing matched seeing her bright smile and the sparkle in her eyes when I returned home after a long day of teaching.

I also think our time together helped heal Nadya from her abusive first marriage. For one thing, she didn't have to worry about having her head pushed inside a refrigerator anymore. For another, she credited me with making her feel whole again. Once, she told a friend, "Harold fixed my broken heart." I could say the same thing about her.

Another blessing was seeing first-hand how God operates when we step out of our comfort zones. Sharing with Mohit and the orphanage children in Bareilly, Kamila in Krasnodar, and the history discussion group in St. Petersburg were indescribable privileges I would have never had while moored inside my safe harbor. I observed Russian and Indian cultures first-hand, experiences few Americans are able to have.

For others, venturing outside the comfort zone may not mean changing location but changing perspective.

If I had my way, every American Christian should be required to spend two years in another country and give a report after their return. Stepping outside my safe area allowed me to have experiences I would have never had otherwise, but more than that, it demonstrated how having a natural curiosity toward people and looking at them as Jesus sees them is much better than isolating inside a tribal cocoon. I listened to people with different ways of thinking without being defensive, and although I didn't always agree with them, it confirmed my idea that the world is more complicated and nuanced than the simplistic views usually portrayed in American media and websites. If the two years away also led people to pray more for other nations and look on others as individuals and not as spiritual projects, so much the better.

This doesn't mean it's necessary to get a visa and a plane ticket for the other side of the world to experience God. Sometimes it may mean talking to someone across the street or a co-worker in the next cubicle. It may mean volunteering, even if your favorite team is playing on TV that night. Often, it's little ways we can bring light to someone that we miss if we're not observant.

The alternative, in my opinion, is to stagnate. A ship anchored safely inside its harbor never makes any progress. Whether the destination is another country or a neighbor across the street, the way to get there is to "go." Our natural instincts, however, say to play it safe. As my wise pastor has said, our prevailing culture is like a tractor beam on *Star Wars*: "You try to get away, but it keeps pulling you back. But unless you escape it, it will destroy you."

Through my five and a half years overseas, I also grew accustomed to uncertainty. When they found out I was an American living in Russia, some Russians told me, "You're a brave man." I didn't feel courageous, but my faith was stretched way more than it had ever been. Everyday life had enough uncertainty, especially with Russia's turbulent economic and political situation during the last half of my stay there. As a result, I had a feeling anything could happen at any time. That intensified on the morning of June 24th, 2016, when news of Nadya's death shook me to the core.

Yet, the "why?" question never bothered me much because God has led me through many difficult times. No one has promised that our lives would be free of pain or trouble. Even though I often felt as if my right arm had been yanked from my body, I relied on God's strength to help me through the waves of grief. A verse that reassured me was Psalm 46:1: "God is our refuge and strength, always ready to help in times of trouble. So we will not fear when earthquakes come and the mountains crumble into the sea." Instead, my main question has not been as much "why?" as "why now?" While I accept death as an inevitable part of life, the timing seemed strange. One of the questions that circulated through my mind was, why did Nadya die just two weeks before her visa interview? I can think of several possible reasons, but who can be certain any of them is correct? I am having to reconcile myself to the fact that I may never know the answers. However, that is alright. I know Who does. And I can bank on His promise: "Trust in the LORD with all your heart and do not lean on your own understanding, in all your ways acknowledge him, and he will make straight your paths" (Proverbs 3:5-6, ESV).

I came to see my reactions to the pain as normal, even the times when I felt like I would burst into tears in the grocery store. I have heard and read several times that a strong relationship exists between grief and love. The more we love a person we have lost, the deeper and more intense our grief will be. Along with that, I realized that Nadya and I would meet again. As Paul wrote in 1 Thessalonians 4:13: "Brothers and sisters, we do not want you to be uninformed about those who sleep in death, so that you do not grieve like the rest of mankind, who have no hope." I may never know the answers to all my questions, but at least for me, I am at peace with that. Life sometimes comes with unanswerable questions. Becoming bitter or disillusioned does nothing to answer them.

Something else I realized after my brain cleared enough to think about what happened during those five and a half years was the importance of reconciliation, both between people and between mankind and God. Nadya and I came out of difficult relationships that ended in divorce. I came to the point that I figured I had no chance to be in a romantic relationship again. At the same time, I knew I couldn't fear love. After surviving an abusive first marriage, Nadya had many of the same reservations. Yet, after we both took a risk, God took our strengths and weaknesses and fashioned us into a strong marriage. Second, God used us as a couple to develop friendships with students and others who may have never heard about Jesus otherwise. Honestly, there were times when Nadya and I thought we should be doing more. However, without a doubt, God was always there. When we had to navigate the bureaucratic paperwork maze to get married. When cashiers sneered and threw change at me. When Nadya smiled and wrapped her arms around my neck for the last time.

After all, she was right. God takes care of crazy people like us.

# ABOUT THE AUTHOR

Harold Campbell worked for 25 years as a reporter and editor at daily newspapers in Kansas and Nebraska. He won a number of Associated Press and state press convention writing awards and, more importantly, gained readers' trust for objectivity and accuracy while preserving a human touch. His freelance articles have appeared in such publications as Baptist Press and *Christianity Today*.

Currently, Campbell tutors writing and history at Georgia Highlands College in Rome, Georgia. He also teaches English as a Second Language online.

*Crazy People Like Us,* his first book, is the story of how Campbell moved to Russia in December 2010 to marry his fiancée, Nadya, and start a new life teaching English as a Foreign Language. Five and a half years later, which includes five months the couple taught English in India, Nadya died unexpectedly after surgery, and Campbell returned to the U.S.

Told from a Christian perspective, *Crazy People Like Us* is more than just a chronicle of an American English teacher's reactions to everyday life in Putin's Russia and his observations of Russian history and culture. Campbell uses the circumstances he experienced to examine such universal themes as reconciliation (both person-to-person and person-to-God), mutual respect between peoples of different cultures, and faith in the middle of uncertainty.

Campbell lives in Cedartown, Georgia, and has two adult children, Tim and Esther, as well as a "Russian daughter," Rita, and "Russian grandsons," William and Robert, who live in St. Petersburg, Russia.

www.ingramcontent.com/pod-product-compliance
Lightning Source LLC
Chambersburg PA
CBHW071438090426
42737CB00011B/1703